"If you place this back on the store shelf or take it home and never read it, you'll regret it. *Wild* is Debbie Alsdorf's best work yet (and I'm not one for doling out author accolades, just so you know), and it's no doubt the result of its message being lived and proved out in her own life. Now that's the kind of book I want to read, as well as the only kind of book I'll recommend."

Julie Barnhill, bestselling author and speaker

"From the first sentence to final page, we are called to live the life most of us have only dreamed of. The impact of Debbie's book upon my life is immeasurable, and I will be forever grateful."

Sue Boldt, women's ministry director,
CrossRoads Community Church, Fairfield, CA

"With rare transparency, Debbie Alsdorf shows us how to have a faith that is bold and vibrant. If you yearn to grow spiritually, you will find *A Different Kind of Wild* to be an excellent read."

Georgia Shaffer, author, *How NOT to Date a Loser*

"Wow! This book is a must-read for everyone who desires to live life wildly different. Instead of being led by our emotions and ever-changing circumstances, Debbie shows how to live a life of confident faith in God's truth. Her honest reflections, practical advice, and God-inspired insights show us a radically different way to live. I'm encouraging every woman at our church to get a copy."

Rachel Johnston, pastor of women's ministry,
Bayside Church, Granite Bay, CA

"Debbie is dynamic in drawing you into an exciting faith adventure that will change your life. Get ready to discover how more of Jesus and less of you will transform your life journey."

Dr. Catherine Hart Weber, therapist, author, speaker, adjunct professor, Fuller Theological Seminary

"In the category of 'it takes one to know one,' I knew I found a kindred (wild) spirit in Debbie Alsdorf. She bravely steps out to show us how to embrace the edges of our lives' ride, the rip-curls of our lives with glorious abandon, knowing that this is the territory where faith becomes reality."

Anita Renfroe, comedian, author

A Different Kind *of* *Wild*

A Different Kind *of* *Wild*

Is Your Faith *too* Tame?

Debbie Alsdorf

Revell

a division of Baker Publishing Group
Grand Rapids, Michigan

Published by Revell
a division of Baker Publishing Group
P.O. Box 6287, Grand Rapids, MI 49516-6287
www.revellbooks.com

Printed in the United States of America

Library of Congress Cataloging-in-Publication Data
Alsdorf, Debbie.
   A different kind of wild : is your faith too tame? / Debbie Alsdorf.
     p. cm.
   Includes bibliographical references (p.   ).
   ISBN 978-0-8007-3366-7 (pbk.)
    1. Christian women—Religious life. I. Title.
BV4527.A457 2009
248.8′43—dc22   2009004859

Dedicated to the Groovy Tuesday Girls—
wild, wacky, and learning to *live up*!
You are my landing place, and I thank God for you.

Contents

Acknowledgments   11

Part One   Developing: Growing Up Spiritually
1. Born to Be Wild   17
2. Wild Women Live Beyond the Norm   31
3. Wild Women Live in Process, Not Perfection   46
4. Wild Women Follow after God   62

Part Two   Daring: Living by a Different Standard
5. Wild Women Choose to Love Others   77
6. Wild Women Forgive and Make Peace   91
7. Wild Women Wear a Different Style   107
8. Wild Women Worry Less and Trust More   119
9. Wild Women Stand Firm in Crisis   129
10. Wild Women Confront Fear with Truth   144

CONTENTS

Part Three Determined: Finding Courage to Follow a New Path

11. Wild Women Have a New Groove   157
12. Wild Women Capture the Sparkle in Life   167

Parting Thoughts   177
Study Guide   179
Notes   205

Acknowledgments

I would like to thank the following people for making a difference in my life as I wrote this book:

Sherrie Short—for living wildly different than the cultural norm as you handled cancer and your "expiration date" with such joy and sparkle. You are missed, and your memory is forever with those who loved you.

Lorri Steer—for living your faith in full color before me.

The women's ministry staff and those in women's ministry leadership at Cornerstone Fellowship—you have embraced this wild ride of development with me. I can't think of a better group of women to grow with than you! Sweet "T," Z-Mamma, Beth Ann, Rose, and Sheree—I apreciate how each of you helped out when I needed time off to write.

Terry Perazza—for being an assistant extraordinaire! Thanks for picking up the slack, from dry cleaning to post office runs to airline tickets—and way too many other things to count. Your handling the details makes so much of what I do possible. I appreciate you! (I think you might even have "angel wings" hidden somewhere!)

My children—from birth and blend—your encouragement means so much to me.

My husband, Ray—you are the wildest blessing of all!

Les Stobbe, my literary agent, and the team at Revell—for believing in the wild path God is calling me to walk in. Thanks for allowing me the blessing of reaching women and encouraging them to learn to live up! A special thanks to Vicki Crumpton for editing my words and making sense of them—now that really is wild! Thanks Vicki!

Do I really dare to let God be to me all that He says He will be?

Oswald Chambers

What if we laid aside life as we knew it—a life where the objective is to secure ourselves, promote ourselves, and indulge our desires? This shift means cooperating with a God who changes us when we finally lay ourselves aside. When we live in his light, we are different than we were before. No longer tame and repressed, we become the passionate, courageous Christ followers that God created us to be. This new life shining in a dark world—this courage from within—this boldness of spirit—is a different kind of wild.

Part

One

Developing

Growing Up Spiritually

Now the Lord is the Spirit, and where the Spirit of the Lord is, there is freedom. And we, who with unveiled faces all reflect the Lord's glory, are being transformed into his likeness with ever-increasing glory, which comes from the Lord, who is the Spirit.

2 Corinthians 3:17–18

The life that Jesus calls us to is absolute craziness to the world.

Chris Tomlin[1]

1

Born to Be Wild

God invites you to join Him.

Henry Blackaby

*Y*ou can become a wild woman. That's right, you heard me—a wild woman. Before you pass out with this book in your hand, let me explain.

I'm not talking about girls gone wild, women acting unruly, or women flipping out on spring break, on summer vacation, or during a midlife crisis. All of those wild women are just acting out. Anyone can act out. This book is a challenge to do something different. This book is about *living up*!

Acting out is when our lives are ruled by emotions, circumstances, and expectations. Sometimes we act out in attitude, and other times our acting out is evident in our actions. In either case, acting out is something we all know how to do; it comes naturally. The Bible calls this acting out of our "self" *living in the flesh*. The result of this lifestyle is bondage to the emotions and expectations that have kept us stuck in our stuff for years.

But what if I told you there was a better way?

Anyone can throw a tantrum and act out. All of us can attend our own pity parties or carry around bad attitudes. But it takes someone whose trust in God is wildly different to choose an upward focus rather than a downward spiral. Keep in mind that each tantrum, each negative response, and each resulting downward spiral starts with a single thing—the choice you make at the time.

- What if I told you that you didn't have to stay stuck?
- What if life could be different?
- Would you like to sign up for calm instead of chaos?
- How about renewed spiritual health to replace exhausting dysfunctional drama?
- What if you could learn a new way to respond to life?
- Why settle for acting out when life could be so much more?

There is a different way to live, and the Bible calls this different life *living in the Spirit*. I affectionately call it *living up*. Living up means a change in focus and direction. Living up moves us from a focus on what we are feeling or what is immediately in front of us to an upward focus on committing our stray thoughts and emotions to God and looking for his Spirit in the midst of us. One is a horizontal view of life and all its immediate problems. The other is the vertical view of God's purpose in our lives in the middle of our everyday realities. Since life doesn't always go our way, learning to live up is a challenge.

In the midst of life circumstances, we easily get frustrated and distracted with the drama of the current moment or event. We settle for acting out while in the frustration of our negative spins. When life distracts us from that upward focus, we appease that wild-child rebel in us by doing our own thing. Let's face it, all of us know how to act out—we have been doing it since we were two.

Admittedly our adult acting out looks a lot different from a two-year-old's. We might not stomp and pout to get our way, but we might close our ears to God and our eyes to sin. When we do this we often find ourselves falling back into old habits and destructive patterns—overeating, overspending, sexual promiscuity, and seemingly innocent flirting with temptation. We might also find ourselves engaging in gossip, loose conversation, little white lies, bitterness, unloving attitudes, frequent anger, and a critical spirit. Our acting out might even become part of who we are and what people expect from us. Many nice Christian women have become experts at acting out.

Most acting out happens in the pressure cooker of real-life circumstances—the kind of circumstances that make you want to throw your arms in the air and proclaim, "I can't take this anymore!" Maybe you even use other choice words that I can't put in print.

Though acting out or living in our self-life is normal and even acceptable in most circles, it's not God's intended best for us. Most women want to live their best life, and I bet you do too. If you want all that God has for you, it's time to come to terms with the power to choose. Your choice in every situation is the difference between a negative or positive outcome. Your choice makes a difference—a big difference.

I want this kind of wild difference to be the exclamation point in every area of my life. I admit I have a lot to learn, and I have finally accepted that it's going to take some time— a lifetime.

Seeing Things Differently

I have always tried my best to get things done as quickly as possible. This included my spiritual growth. I wanted to read a few books, memorize a few verses, and know that I'd arrived. But a few years ago God showed me a different perspective.

I was complaining, once again, about my circumstances: "O Lord, I am so over this stuff! Why do we keep coming back to these same old problems? I am worn out and tired of trials, tests, and the stuff that is supposed to shape me. Right now I think maturity and character building is overrated!"

Gently he spoke to my heart. *"Debbie, I want to make you wild for me."*

"Hmm . . . wild? What does that mean? Do you want me to wear leopard clothes, bungee jump at the county fair, dye my hair hot pink? What in the world does being wild for you mean? And what does wild have to do with the mess I'm in today?"

I had once heard WILD used as an acronym for Women in Leadership Development, so I immediately tried applying this new wild nudge from God to my position of leadership at our local church. Our leadership teams were growing and could use a face-lift, so I assumed that was why God was speaking to me about getting wild. That was it: a fresh season for the women in leadership—wild.

But I couldn't end my thought process with just that. Once again I felt the stirring within me: *"Debbie, I want to make you wild for me."*

"I heard you, Lord, but what do you mean?"

Clearly I was being called to attention. I had a sense that God wanted to make a change in my life and that it had to do with me as an individual more than it had to do with me as a leader in women's ministry. Slowly, God continued to speak to my heart—and he reminded me that before I was ever a leader, I was born to be his. Before I ever said yes to him, he knew I was born for the purpose of being shaped by him. He desired to change me in order to fulfill the plans he had already prepared for me to walk in (see Eph. 2:10).

The God of all creation was getting my attention. He wanted my complete surrender. He called me to follow him in a lifelong pursuit and process of spiritual development. He wasn't interested in what I could bring to the table—he was more interested in developing me along the lines of his Son. And this could happen only if I daily answered the call to come to him.

In a recent Internet devotional, Rick Warren said, "Becoming like Christ is a long, slow process of growth. Spiritual maturity is neither instant nor automatic; it is a gradual, progressive development that will take the rest of your life. God is far more interested in who you are than in what you do. We are human beings, not human doings. You must make a countercultural decision to focus on becoming more like Jesus. Otherwise other forces like peers, parents, co-workers, and the culture will try to mold you into their image."[1]

I think what God was trying to say to me was that I needed to make a decision that was contrary to the mission statements and plans of this culture. God's plan was to make me more like himself, and that would take a countercultural decision on my part. It would take a shift in focus, mission, and life path.

That's quite a development plan.

The Bible warns, "Don't become so well-adjusted to your culture that you fit into it without even thinking. Instead, fix your attention on God. You'll be changed from the inside out. . . . Unlike the culture around you, always dragging you down to its level of immaturity, God brings the best out of you, develops well-formed maturity in you" (Rom. 12:2 Message).

Oh, I was beginning to get it. God wanted to develop well-formed maturity in me. This spiritual maturity would replace the immaturity that causes me to act out rather than live up. I started to get the message loud and clear. It's about embracing the process of life and growth with him rather than striving for personal goals of self-focused perfection. In a world that is all about getting ourselves "together" (perfection), this new way to view and frame life (process of development) was certainly a wild idea.

Rick Warren said: "Sadly, a quick review of many popular Christian books reveals that many believers have abandoned living for God's great purposes and settled for personal fulfillment and emotional stability. That is narcissism, not discipleship. Jesus did not die on the cross just so we could live comfortable, well-adjusted lives. His purpose is far deeper: he wants to make us like himself before he takes us to heaven. This is our greatest privilege, our immediate responsibility, and our ultimate destiny."[2]

The idea of accepting my self and my life while in the process of growth, rather than the race to perfection, brought me immediate peace. So, for the purpose of this book, WILD refers to being *women in lifelong development*:

Women
In
Lifelong
Development

The key is *lifelong development*. There are no overnight spiritual success stories. We are on a journey with God that is deeper than perceived perfection or the rush of instant success. Each day the pages of life are turned, and line by line our story unfolds. It is a process.

> **process:** a series of steps toward a desired
> end

Why Become a Wild Woman?

Recently someone asked me if I ever felt anxious, tempted to give up, or even discouraged. I was surprised that she had to wonder. I smiled and said, "Yes, all of the above, but it's getting better all the time, because as I am growing to know Jesus more, I am falling away from fear and growing deeper in faith."

"Were you always like this?"

"No, definitely not!" I went on to tell her, "The good news is Jesus changes people."

As we grow in Christ, we change and become different. As we are changed we become more daring—daring to live in the truth of what we believe. It's exciting when we begin experiencing God and his Word rather than just talking about it. The book of James says, "Faith without works is dead" (2:20 NKJV). Many of us have learned to live like we are dead. Here's a news flash: dead girls aren't wild; they're lifeless, useless, and buried in self. But women who are alive in Christ and actively living up in the truth of God's Word are passionate, free, unconventional, and courageous.

> **passionate:** expressing strong emotion and excitement

> **free:** not confined or obstructed; open, unreserved, unbound

> **unconventional:** not conforming to the standard of culture

> **courageous:** brave, bold, daring, adventurous

We were born to surrender to the process of his Spirit working in us; this is different from most people's mission statement for life. And that's what being wild is all about— the radically authentic life that says yes to the call to move outside of the norm and live in the wild terrain of faith, hope, and love—for real.

When I wrote *Deeper*, I began with the assumption, based on my own experience, that most women want something more—and that we just aren't sure how to get it. We try to find that elusive "it" in everything around us: in people; in being pretty, perfect, and polished; or in any success we can attain and hold on to.

We end up on the perfection and performance track, and though we are huffing and puffing through life, we still end up empty—chasing, longing, and looking for something better.

The idea of something more or something different can be a bit scary. We don't know what to expect. We fear having all the fun and personality zapped out of us in the name of spirituality. We worry we will become robots. This unknown scares most of us away from living wildly abandoned to the God who made us. And so we settle. We settle for less than what God has created us for. We are afraid to let go, so we hold on for dear life to our own attempts at making a good life for ourselves.

Some assume that if they wildly abandon themselves to God, they will be expected to have a holy and serious posture—bland, reserved, and, well, boring—when their real personality is happy, bubbly, and a bit silly. We go as far as thinking we might have to spend our days wearing suits, pearls, or church-lady clothes, when what we really want to do is throw on some leopard heels and get a groove on.

Real Women in the Real World

It's time to say we're done with fake people and flimsy gods. Now's the time to be done with being hypocritical—saying we are happy when we're sad, saying we're filled with faith when we're filled with fear, and acting like we aren't rebellious when we know we're recovering rebels at heart. Women today are real, and they want to have faith in a real God. We want to know and experience a God big enough to handle our stresses, our shortcomings, and our lives in the real world. We need to know how to live in a world filled with the dangerous terrain of disappointment, heartache, broken promises, and shattered dreams. God holds out something more to us every day when he invites us to join him. And now the question is: are you ready—really ready for more?

So what's a girl to do? Personally, I think it's time to get *wild*! It's time to grow deeper and reach higher. It's time to learn what it means to *live up*! And because living up does not come naturally to most of us, it's a lifestyle to be learned—a life based on living, breathing, and moving in step with God's Spirit within us. A life that is rooted in the vertical connection of looking up, praying up, and living up to the standards that God has put before us in the Bible.

Learning to *live up* establishes faith, enriches our sense of purpose, and lifts our sagging spirits when life gets too hard. *Living up* involves wild choices made out of obedience to God. *Living up* challenges us to go under the knife—not plastic surgery but process development, as the knife of God's Word penetrates the deepest part of us with truth. This new wild is about taking our lives back from anything that holds us back and reclaiming the lives that God has created us for. It's about becoming women who dare to live differently— living in the faith we profess and daring to choose to live what we say we believe. It's daring to say what we believe and live what we say!

I admit it's funny that a woman in her fifties is talking about going wild. I guess it's logical to wonder if I've gone off the deep end or if I am in the middle of a midlife crisis! Or could it be that I am so blown away by what I am learning that I have to share it with others?

I'll claim the last one. As I look back at my life, I realize how much precious time I have wasted—totally wasted—on living somewhere in between everything I am and everything

I was created to be. It struck me a few years back that there are no dress rehearsals. Today is all I have to live. The current scene I am living is being aired live, with no second takes. Today counts for eternity.

Born for the Big Picture

We were born to live up instead of settling for being dragged down by our emotions or circumstances. I guess you could say we were born to be wild! We were:

> born for purposes greater than ourselves,
> born to glorify the Father,
> born to love God with every part of us,
> born to love others with God's love that is within us,
> born to hear the voice of God,
> born for something greater than we now know,
> born to be in the processing solution of God's Spirit,
> born to be changed from glory to glory,
> born to answer the call to "come" to Christ and then live by the instruction to "follow" after him,
> born to live by faith—not by sight,
> born to live out what we really believe, even when others call us crazy.

Does This Line Up with God's Word?

Every time I sense God speaking to my heart, I turn to Scripture to see if what I am sensing lines up with the truth of God's Word. There is power in going back to basics and learning to live in them. For the past eighteen years, this returning to what I thought I knew but didn't know how to live in has become my pursuit. Before I sit down to read the

Bible, I ask God to make it new to me—fresh, relevant, and practical for my life today as a real woman who desires to learn to live up and walk with God.

It's easy to skim or skip over the basic passages we have read before. Please don't. Reading and hearing is one thing—internalizing and living out is another. Let God's Word speak to you. It's more life-changing than me trying to convince you.

Take a moment and read this passage from Colossians. It is Paul's prayer for the church:

> We haven't stopped praying for you, asking God to give you wise minds and spirits attuned to his will, and so acquire a thorough understanding of the ways in which God works. We pray that you'll live well for the Master, making him proud of you as you work hard in his orchard. As you learn more and more how God works, you will learn how to do your work. We pray that you'll have the strength to stick it out over the long haul—not the grim strength of gritting your teeth but the glory-strength God gives. It is strength that endures the unendurable and spills over into joy, thanking the Father who makes us strong enough to take part in everything bright and beautiful that he has for us.
>
> God rescued us from dead-end alleys and dark dungeons. He's set us up in the kingdom of the Son he loves so much, the Son who got us out of the pit we were in, got rid of the sins we were doomed to keep repeating. . . . Everything got started in him and finds its purpose in him. He was there before any of it came into existence and holds it all together right up to this moment. . . .
>
> You yourselves are a case study of what he does. At one time you all had your backs turned to God, thinking rebellious thoughts of him, giving him trouble every chance you got. But now, by giving himself completely at the Cross, actually dying for you, Christ brought you over to God's side and put your lives together, whole and holy in his presence. You don't walk away from a gift like that!
>
> Colossians 1:9–14, 16–17, 21–23 Message

What did Paul pray for them that relates to us? Paul asked God to:

- give them wise minds and spirits attuned to his will;
- give them the wisdom and understanding to recognize the ways God works;
- enable them to live well for the Master;
- give them strength to stick it out over the long haul.

This is pretty wild stuff. It all boils down to one wild prayer: *"Less of me and more of thee"* (see John 3:30).

Let's close this thought by continuing with truth, as the apostle Paul goes on to tell them:

> For by him all things were created: things in heaven and on earth, visible and invisible, whether thrones or powers or rulers or authorities; all things were created by him and for him. He is before all things, and in him all things hold together.
>
> Colossians 1:16–17

Can you hear what Paul is saying about how big God is? Do you get a glimpse of your purpose as you realize that you were created for a God who made everything? And what about the awesome fact that God holds you together this very moment? God desires to speak truth to your heart, singing a song of love and redemption over you. Will you say yes to going deeper and reaching higher? Will you dare to say yes to the call to be wild? Will you say yes to a different focus and a countercultural way of addressing your life's greatest needs?

In the book *Crazy Love*, Francis Chan says, "To be brutally honest, it doesn't really matter what place you find yourself in right now. Your part is to bring Him glory—whether eating a sandwich on a lunch break, drinking coffee at 12:04 a.m. so you can stay awake to study, or watching your four-month-old take a nap. The point of your life is to point to Him. Whatever you are doing God wants to be glorified, because this whole thing is His. It is His movie, His world, His gift."[3]

Ah . . . yes, the point of our lives is to point to him.

Thinking we could be changed into his image is a wild thought.

He is asking us to come—and then to follow. Will you answer that call? Following Christ and living up is radical and different. This difference is a new way to be wild!

Wild Strategies for Growing Up Spiritually

Look Up

- Identify the ways you typically act out.
- Imagine how different living up would be.

Pray Up

- Pray the wild prayer: "Less of me and more of thee."
- Ask God to show you the areas in your life that are immature.
- Pray for God to shape you and make you more like him.

Live Up

- Choose the wild way—living up instead of acting out.
- Try incorporating the idea of living up instead of acting out into circumstances as they arise by finding a "truth verse" that counters the thing you want to do based on your own feelings and emotions.
- Decide to live by a mission statement that might be countercultural but biblically correct.
- Embrace the process of growth and get excited about learning to live a different way.

Questions for Reflection on the Wild Life

1. When you think of "acting out," what comes to your mind?
2. Read Galatians 5:19–21. How does this passage relate to the idea of acting out?
3. What does "living up" mean to you?
4. Read Colossians 1:9–23. What part of this passage is most meaningful to you and why?
5. Do you think you were born to be a Woman in Lifelong Development (WILD)?

2

Wild Women Live
Beyond the Norm

Life—the Christian Journey—should be infused with exploration and discovery and yes,
fun! God is untamed, unbound; there are no
limits to what He will do in our lives if we
are willing to let Him work through us and
in us.

Michelle Borquez[1]

*W*hat's normal? I suppose normal is in the eye of the
beholder. Normal for one person might not be what
the norm is for the next. The dictionary defines normal as
the expected or usual condition. All of us have our own usual
condition—our habits, practices, and ways of viewing life.
Our normal is how we live on a regular daily basis. For many
Christian women, normal has become stuffing our stuff into
a box and acting out our faith in a masquerade that is killing

the authentic intimacy that God calls us to. Rather than living in the excitement of spiritual discovery, our normal is living a predictable life based on what we feel, see, and experience. This is not a life of faith—but this is the normal Christian life for many of us.

What's your normal? Is it anger, living out the dysfunction of your past, or continuing in the sin that you are comfortable with? Is it unhealthy relationships, unbending attitudes, and pride? Is it selfishness, self-focus, and lack of concern for other's opinions? Is it insecurity, fear of failure, or fear of rejection? Is it feeling you will never measure up or be enough? Is your normal running away or falling apart every time things get too hard?

All of us have a normal, and it's the way we have learned to process and respond to life. The other day while in a thrift shop I saw a plaque that read, "Our natural and normal life is a formidable obstacle to our spiritual life." How true this is. My normal, emotion-based life that is holding on to self-preservation will keep me from full surrender to God. A life of faith is the opposite of a life of existing by feelings.

My normal has been changed. What used to be life as usual for me is now a thing of the past. This is good, because my life as usual was less than God's best for me. Rather than living a life of faith, I lived a life of fear. My fears manifested themselves in insecurities. These insecurities would stop me from doing things, stop me from having healthy relationships, and stop me from embracing God's love for me.

Often we aren't happy with life as it is, so we try to change people, control circumstances, and manipulate the outcome of situations. And when we haven't been successful, we have learned how to act out—usually due to fear and the helpless feeling of things being out of our control.

Before I realized the implications of belonging to God, I spent my life living in fear. Living in fear made control a part of my normal reasoning and activity. Daring to live a true life of faith rather than trying to control my environment was far too hard. Besides, I felt that I was already living up and doing what was expected by attending church, reading my Bible, and participating in small groups. I even served in many ministry positions. But despite the flurry of spiritual activities, something seemed to be blocking me from being able to rise above and beyond my circumstances and trust God. I guess you could say I didn't know how to really live up; I didn't know that living up was far more than showing up when the church doors opened. My faith was real, but it was disordered and unfocused. It didn't affect the realities or practical places of my life, because I continued to live by my emotions, which were dictated by my current circumstances—good and bad. My faith was not wild; it was tame.

tame: subdued, repressed, depressed, shut, restrained, silenced

A faith that is silenced by fear is a depressed, tame faith. Fear gives way to the flesh, and the flesh gives way to acting out—time and time again. Acting out can be as simple as clamming up in response to someone's attitude or reacting to a situation with uncontrolled emotion or anger. Acting out can look like pride rather than humility, dislike rather than love, drama rather than deliberate peace, or negativity rather than joy. Yes, it's easy to see that acting out is all around us; it's part of what we expect; it's part of how we live. Living in our self is how we are wired—the human flesh part of us. But the new software of the Holy Spirit installed within us promises the power and programming to live according to a different menu of options.

As I lived life on an emotional roller coaster, the internal pain of my circumstances became a megaphone for me over and over again. God was calling me to listen to his voice. Sometimes I listened and other times I didn't. When God creatively got my attention, I finally listened. I heard a call to change. A call to live a life above and beyond my normal way of living. I realized that coming to Jesus was a vitally important step. The next step was just as important: learning to follow him throughout my life.

Lately I've been encouraging a friend to live up. She has been hurt by unfair and unreasonable accusations. And just like any other person who has been hurt, she was ready to "act out." Each new verbal stab from Christians who were judging her unfairly made her want to do some pretty ugly things. I reminded her that she already knew how to act out, but God wanted to teach her something new. He was going to teach her to live up in a different place.

One day, in a pool of hurt, she called me for prayer. "Will you please pray for me right now? I am so hurt, so broken, so mad. I want to scream! This whole thing is so unfair, and I'm not even able to defend myself."

As her voice cracked, giving way to tears, she squeaked out, "Debbie, tell me how to live up in this mess—how do I live up? What do I do now?"

This circumstance was real and painful and seemed unfair. She had a choice to make. Would she rely on God's power and presence in the mess, or would she take the easier road of letting it all hang out?

We walked through three important steps that are not the typical or normal first reaction for any of us when we are hurt:

1. Take responsibility—ask God to forgive you for your part in the situation and to show you what that is.
2. Take action—seek to live in truth by finding out what Scripture says about handling the situation in the Spirit rather than the flesh.
3. Take time out—commit your way to God and ask him for the power to yield to the Spirit within you.

In my friend's case, she realized that her "Spirit choice" would be to choose peace, love, and longsuffering over dissension and factions. She could easily go about causing dissension—we all know how to gossip, seek attention with our stories of hurt, and so on—but that is the flesh (Galatians 5 speaks of the Spirit life as contrary to the flesh life). Each day for about two weeks, she chose the higher road, committing her hurt to God and praying the wild prayer, "Jesus, less of me and more of thee." She made it through, and God turned things around in the end. Thankfully she didn't act out and didn't destroy relationships or burn bridges in the process. Her actions were far from her typical normal pattern of dealing with life and relationships. But this time her situation, though hard, brought amazing joy as she realized how close to her God was on this journey of discovery.

Life is filled with these kinds of things—daily annoyances, hurts, and disruptions. From our marriages to our places of employment, from neighborhood to church, from young to old—we all have circumstances that must be dealt with. The Christian life is an intimate encounter with Christ, and our response to that intimacy of relationship is putting faith into action. And in real life that means learning to live in the Spirit's power instead of the normal acting out of our selves.

Keep in mind that acting out always starts with an emotional response, and each response begins with an emotional choice. Contrary to acting out, living up always starts with a spiritual response, and each response begins with an upward focused choice that we often wrestle with a bit before fully surrendering our will to it. In my friend's case, she wrestled with not wanting unity but desiring for others to feel hurt the way they made her hurt. Once she gave all her hurt to God, she realized how immature she was being and chose something different—not normal but wild.

35

What Is Your Wild Place?

I have begun asking myself what I'm wild (passionately en-thusiastic) about. I come up with silly things like shopping, decorating, eating, socializing, my children, my husband . . . you get the idea. I realized I was wild about many things, all of which were good and normal for me to be passionate about. But now God was calling me to a different norm—a place where I would be called to be wild in surrender, wild in devotion, wild in service, and wild in following what the New Testament outlines for us, as believers, to experience, live in, and follow. I heard the call, that's for sure—I just wasn't certain what being wild for Jesus looked like.

Wild Scares Us

Some of you may remember the 1960s rock band Steppenwolf and their hit song "Born to Be Wild." With the song as the title cut for the *Easy Rider* movie soundtrack, the idea of being wild became associated with motorcycles and speed. It was a song of adventure—wild, crazy, unbridled adventure. And though many have rocked out to this classic rock song, the truth is, wildness scares us.

Being wild means being rebellious, unpredictable, foolish, dangerous, crazy, or out of control. Wild animals are kept in cages, wild people are locked behind bars, wild celebri-ties are on magazine covers or in fancy rehab centers, and wild children are disciplined by exasperated parents. Being wild gets us in trouble. For most of us, being wild is unac-ceptable. We like to keep wild at a distance and warn our children to stay away from wild people, wild driving, and wild activities.

But what if there is a different kind of wild? What if being wild could be turned to mean positive living instead of the typical rebellious, dangerous, crazy, irresponsible, or destruc-tive path that usually defines being wild?

The Bible is filled with wild-faith people—those who took a different path and wild risks while trusting God. In ancient times, God spoke and people heard. Wild? Yes! But it gets even wilder. The people not only heard but also followed the voice and path of God.

Think how wild it must have seemed when Noah built an ark or when people walked through the Red Sea. What about when the walls of Jericho came falling down after wild-faith people marched around the city for seven days? How about walking on water? Now, that's not just wild; it's downright crazy.

What about John the Baptist dressed in camel's hair, eating locusts, and proclaiming the coming of the Messiah? He was proclaiming something that no one had yet seen—but he was wild enough to proclaim what he believed. Do you think it seemed a little wild that the Son of God was born in a stable to an unwed mother who had never been intimate with a man? How about Jesus changing the water into wine—how wild is that? Imagine for a moment being the woman at the well encountering a stranger who knew your secret shame and all your past relationships—a man who said he was the Messiah, God's Son. Crazy? Wild?

Is all this normal? I don't think so.

Is it wild? You'd better believe it.

Becoming a Wild-Faith Woman

Maybe it's just me, but the thought of relating to a God that I cannot see with human eyes is a bit wild, and sometimes it seems a little crazy. Even more amazing is that he's a God who is all-knowing and personally involved with human lives; he is fully devoted to those he has created, constantly committed to the welfare of his people, sovereign over the future of humankind, and readily connected to those who will answer the call to come to him. Is faith in this kind of

God a little over the top—a little on the wild side? It's daring, isn't it?

Although wild is usually dangerous in nature, I am beginning to think that becoming a wild-faith woman is the answer to the dangerous world we live in. No, it's not ordinary; it's not the norm. But that's what wild is—wild is living outside of the norm. We live in a world where wild is defined as anything that is untamed, unknown, and not uniform. I think it's time to redefine wild and turn our secret bent toward acting out into a daring commitment to living up.

Here's how Webster's dictionary defines *wild*:

- going beyond normal or conventional bounds
- extravagant
- not subject to restraint
- passionately enthusiastic
- strong desire or emotion
- a free or natural state of existence
- out of control
- living in a life or existence that is not tame

God calls us to a different kind of wild. A life without the restraints of human understanding but rather a life alive to faith in the mighty power of God.

- Going beyond normal or conventional bounds
    Living as the people of God—1 Peter 2:9–10
- Not subject to restraint
    Not being conformed to the world—Romans 12:1–2
- Passionately enthusiastic
    Christ's love compels me to live for him—2 Corinthians 5:14–15
- Strong desire or emotion
    The life I live, I live by faith—Galatians 2:20

- A free or natural state of existence
  Experiencing a new freedom in Christ—Galatians 5:1
- Out of control
  No longer trusting in my own understanding—Proverbs 3:5–6
- Living in a life or existence that is not tame
  Courageously holding on to the hope I profess—Hebrews 10:23

Rethinking Normal

The wild-faith people in the Bible were just like you and me. We read the accounts of their lives and think that they were different and that we could never have the same type of relationship with God that they had. But it simply is not true. God desires for us to live as people belonging to him. Take a look at what Scripture says about this:

> But you are a chosen people, a royal priesthood, a holy nation, a people belonging to God, that you may declare the praises of him who called you out of darkness into his wonderful light. Once you were not a people, but now you are the people of God.
>
> 1 Peter 2:9–10

It is not normal, in the culture we live in, to live as a chosen royal priest when you are a regular neighbor, friend, and co-worker. It is acceptable to live set apart if you live in a monastery or convent. But Scripture tells us we are all, as his children, to be living in his light, set apart to be the people of God. This is not the norm. Recognizing the truth of who we are is the turning point.

Here is an example of normal in our world today:

For although they knew God, they neither glorified him as God nor gave thanks to him, but their thinking became futile and their foolish hearts were darkened. Although they claimed to be wise, they became fools and exchanged the glory of the immortal God for images made to look like mortal man. . . . They exchanged the truth of God for a lie, and worshiped and served created things rather than the Creator.

Romans 1:21–23, 25

Remember that Paul instructs us in Romans 12:2 to no longer be conformed to the culture we live in. Wild? Yes, but it's God's instruction to us, for our good, growth, and best.

- Think of the world we live in—what is normal in our culture?
- Think of the circle of friends you hang with—what is the normal way of relating?
- Think of the laws that are passed—what has become normal in our living?
- Think of the magazines we look at—what is normal in our expectations?
- Think of the debt people are in—what is normal in our spending?

When I process what is normal in the world I live in, I think that learning to live beyond the realm of what has become normal or conventional is probably a pretty good idea. It makes me realize that learning to live up is important. I admit it is safe and predictable to live within the confines of the culturally approved. But I don't see that in the Bible. Instead, I see people like the apostle Paul, who turned his life around after God stopped him—or blinded him—in his tracks on the road to Damascus. Paul's normal became a thing of the past, and a wild devotion to Christ became his new life.

If the examples in the Bible are meant to guide my path as a believer today, then living out my days as one committed to

Christ falls into the range defined as wild. Going beyond what is normal in our culture, living beyond what we can see and feel, and living outside of the "normal" dysfunctions of our human nature—this is wild indeed. The Bible calls it faith. And all those who went before us, who lived in faith, who lived wildly unpredictable—yet trusting—lives are examples for us today.

I never cease to be amazed that God selected me, imperfect me, to be on his team. I often forget this basic truth, but I am finding the need to keep returning to it. When I live as one who has been selected, then I live differently—with humility, appreciation, conviction, and a different compass.

Matthew Henry wrote, "All true Christians are a chosen generation, they all make one family, a sort and species of people distinct from the common world. . . . This dignity of Christians is not natural to them, their first state is darkness, but they are called out of the darkness by Christ. Their position with God: deeply loved. Their condition in the world: strangers and pilgrims. They should not give in to the lusts of the country they are passing through."[2]

We are told that God selected us. And not only did he select us, but we belong to him, and we belong to a new family—the family of believers. I don't know about you, but I think this is pretty wild. Try explaining this to the people you work with. They might look at you the same way someone might have looked at Noah. *What? You're doing what? Building an ark?*

Instead of building an ark, you find yourself explaining that you live your life differently because you are called to follow after God. As your co-workers get that glazed look in their eyes, you go on with your story: "Once I didn't know him, but now that I do, I have a new life." You might even tell them they can too. "Really?" one says with raised brow.

She didn't realize you were different until you took the wild step of proclaiming the truth. You have just crossed the line of what is politically and socially correct or normal in our culture. You admitted that you were a woman of faith—yes, you were wild enough to tell the truth about who you are because of Christ. You even dared to admit that you were born again.

Stepping Outside the Pink Box

Daring to step outside the normal, culturally acceptable box feels a bit weird but is exciting. Far too many of us have been conditioned to live in our little pink boxes of perfection: pleasing people, being socially correct—though sometimes spiritually wrong. We work hard at trying to perfect every move we make. This sense of control helps us feel good about ourselves and about our lives. But in this box of perfection, we are stifled and become stale in our faith. Rather than grow, we shrink within the self-imposed walls of trying to be sugar, spice, and everything nice.

Remember the nursery rhyme? Little boys are made of frogs, snails, and puppy dog tails, and little girls are made of sugar and spice and everything nice. Think about it. What pictures come to mind when you think of the two?

I get the mental picture of muddy-fingered, stinky little boys running through fields laughing—having the time of their lives. They are adventurous. But when I think of the little girls, I envision pretty princesses sitting silently in their pink fluffy tutus, hands folded in their laps, sweetly smiling while waiting for their next performance. They are still, and with the exception of a polite giggle here and there, they are silent. Little girls are confined in a world of watching their steps—or, as the nursery rhyme says, being sugar, spice, and everything nice.

For boys there is adventure. But there is no adventure in the fluff of trying to be perfectly put together. There is nothing wild about the pink box. The only thing wild about it is the insanity of trying to conform to the culturally accepted standard of being little sweethearts. It's time for us big little girls to grow up. We might not want to, but we have to if we want to live different lives.

The apostle Paul speaks of this: "When I was a child, I talked like a child, I thought like a child, I reasoned like a child. When I became a man, I put childish ways behind me" (1 Cor. 13:11). How many of us are still talking, thinking, and reasoning from the immature place of that little girl of the past? Sure, it might be acceptable to everyone around you, but is it God's best? Do you think you will find the radical shift in life that you long for by living according to the same patterns you always have lived in? You probably won't. Neither will I.

In order for me to live differently, I will have to put that little girl who is sitting waiting for the next performance to rest—and begin to live as the woman of God that his Word says I am.

I want to paint the box red, or maybe hot pink, or perhaps a little leopard print will do. I want to laugh—and laugh out loud. I want to live—accepting that sometimes real life gets messy. I want to smile at everyone I meet—strangers, enemies, and those I love. I want to say what I mean—and live what I say. I want to trust God to sort through my processing, and then I want to run—faster and harder than I ever have before.

I am in the race of life, and I want to live it, run it, embrace it—every moment of it. Yes, I am ready to get wild about life in Christ. How about you?

If you said yes, then I'm going to have to be honest with you—there is some good news and some bad news. Which would you like first? Well, I'll cut to the chase and give you the bad news. Ready?

The Bad News

Getting wild about living requires letting go of the wheel of your life, and this can be scary and hard. Maybe you have calluses and white knuckles from hanging on so tightly to the wheel of your life. You will have to let go and let God have it all. Then you will have to acknowledge the self-imposed restrictions that have held you back and kept you down. There will be changes in attitude, shifts in lifestyle, and new choices to be made. Ready for the good news?

The Good News

The flip side is not just good news—it's great! The God of the universe becomes your driver. It's less stressful with Jesus at the wheel, and it's more fun because you can enjoy the ride, take in the sights, and trust in the destination. There is real adventure ahead, and it can be found in embracing the process of being changed by God. This acceptance enables us to learn from our mistakes, trust God with messy pieces, and practice obedience. This new wild surrender will enable us to experience changes in our attitude, shifts in our lifestyle, and the freedom to make choices that affect everything from our moods to our daily relationships. All of this represents change—the change of being in the developing process with the God who created us. And living in the process is the good news—because living in the process means being in relationship with Jesus.

Ken Gire writes, "Because Jesus promised to disclose himself intimately to us, I have every confidence that in some way or another he will make good on that promise. The anticipation heightens my awareness to the ordinary moments of my day. Remarkable things happen when I pay attention. Here and there I actually do see something of his presence. Now and then I really do hear something of his voice."[3]

Sadly, this kind of passionate focus on our Lord is not as normal as it should be. It's time to move beyond the norm and learn to pay attention to his voice and be committed to following his commands. In this place we will begin to experience God in the ordinary moments of life.

Wild women live beyond the norm—and experience God. He is asking us to come—and then to follow—and then to experience his presence. He is asking us to put on that royal robe and step out into this world as his daughters. Will you change your thrift shop rags for the priceless crown?

Wild Strategies for Living Beyond the Norm

Look Up

- Think of your most recent daily challenge. Did you ask yourself what Jesus would have you do in it, or did you handle business as usual, doing it your way?

Pray Up

- Ask God to show you the reality of who you are in him. Pray that this reality will make such an impact within you that your new normal will be to live completely sold out and wildly surrendered to him.

Live Up

- Take accountability for bad attitudes and actions before they take control of you.

Questions for Reflection on the Wild Life

1. What is your normal?
2. Read 1 Peter 2:9 and Romans 1:21–24 and note the contrasts.
3. Is it hard for you to embrace a royal reality?
4. How does thinking about being "the people of God" affect you?
5. Do you think that you would live differently if you remembered that you belong to God and not this world, other people, or yourself?

3

Wild Women Live
in Process,
Not Perfection

Perfectionists often appear to be highly moti-
vated, but their motivations usually come from
a desperate attempt to avoid the low self-esteem
they experience when they fail. This tendency
suffocates joy and creativity.

Robert S. McGee

*I*t was just an ordinary Saturday. I puttered around the
house, played with the dogs, joked around with my adult
kids, and then planned to get ready for my friend's memorial
service. My husband and I had looked forward to celebrating
Sherrie's life with all her friends and family. We expected a
big crowd and a beautiful homecoming to honor a longtime
member of our church community. As I goofed around with
my kids in the family room, I suddenly felt like I had been

shot in the leg by a sniper hiding in a corner with a silencer on his gun. Before I could think about what hit me, I was down on the ground.

The kids thought I was joking around when they heard high-pitched noises coming out of me. I wasn't screaming; there were no real words but rather intense shrill peeps coming from me as a cry for help. They thought I was laughing so hard that I could hardly breathe, but I was actually hurting so much that I could barely speak. Something had gone terribly wrong.

Finally, I was able to yelp out for help, and when I couldn't get myself up, everyone knew this was no laughing matter. Quickly my husband and son picked me up and carried me to the car, and instead of going to Sherrie's service, we headed to the hospital.

God has plans to shape us in the midst of our circumstances. I don't always understand it, and I often don't like the things that throw me into another round of learning. But that is what surrendering to living beyond myself is all about: it's agreeing to say yes to the process of being a Woman in Lifelong Development. To be developed, I have to go through the process of learning, stretching, growing—and yes, even sometimes having my life totally interrupted because God has plans to shape me in the middle of my circumstances.

Life has a way of catching us at inopportune times and leaving us frustrated with the way things are. The Bible often calls these interruptions trials—and fiery ones at that. The Bible also calls these interruptions tests, as our faith is put through a sieve with which God filters out the icky parts of us as his Spirit leads us into maturity. We may not like it, but it's God's way, and it would be good for us to embrace it.

Not Conformed to This World

Most of us have learned to live by worldly standards. As the apostle Paul put it:

It wasn't so long ago that you were mired in that old stagnant life of sin. You let the world, which doesn't know the first thing about living, tell you how to live. You filled your lungs with polluted unbelief, and then exhaled disobedience. We all did it, all of us doing what we felt like doing, when we felt like doing it.

Ephesians 2:1–3 Message

Though we are believers, many of us still let the world or the wiring of our fleshly human nature shape our lives. We do what we feel like doing when we feel like doing it. God is calling us to a wild shift. Instead of doing our own thing, we can learn to live God's way.

Only a wild woman could embrace life's challenges, interruptions, and uncomfortable circumstances. The apostle James lived a courageously different life and pointed others in the direction of faith and trust. He viewed life's interruptions as a gift:

Consider it a sheer gift, friends, when tests and challenges come at you from all sides. You know that under pressure, your faith-life is forced into the open and shows its true colors. So don't try to get out of anything prematurely. Let it do its work so you become mature and well-developed, not deficient in any way.

James 1:2–4 Message

Imagine being able to consider yourself fortunate or to view it as pure joy when life hits you up with troubles. Now that is wild, isn't it?

Though I planned on attending Sherrie's memorial, I ended up in the hospital instead. After a few hours in the local emergency room, I was diagnosed with a ruptured calf muscle, an injury that usually happens to athletes—which I am not. I was given a wheelchair and prescribed several weeks, which turned into several months, of complete inactivity. The first few days the pain was so intense that it stole every ounce of my energy and attention. My lower leg became black and swollen, pulsating with any movement. After a few days of that kind of intensity, I had the challenge of adjusting to pain, immobility, and a new view from the wheelchair.

Each day before leaving for work, my husband would get me ready for the day. He would wheel me up to the kitchen table where my coffee and breakfast were waiting, kiss me on the cheek, and leave for work. From that point everything began to get emotionally dark, and I began to fight that old enemy, depression, that tries to sweep me away with discouragement, self-pity, or fear. Someone once told me that all pity parties are catered by Satan himself. I knew that if I accepted the invitation to the pity party, I would begin to spiral emotionally, which would end up affecting me spiritually. I imagined myself sitting in that chair crying, feeling lonely, accusing God of not being with me, or worse yet, accusing God of not even loving me enough to protect me. I knew I was capable of some pretty ugly negative stuff. Since I was just hanging on by a thread, I decided to decline Satan's invitation to the pity party. I fought discouragement and going into a pit of depression by reading the Psalms aloud. I began praising God every hour on the hour, thanking him for loving me and being with me.

And though I was determined to praise God rather than pity myself, the truth is, I did not want to be developed. I was too busy. I had places to go, people to see, ministry to do. I had anticipated a full and wonderful spring speaking season. And quite frankly, I wasn't happy about changing those plans so I could become more mature! As far as I was concerned, maturity was way overrated. But realizing the only other alternative was self-pity and the dark hole that Satan wanted to trap me in, I made a choice to let go and learn whatever it was God wanted to teach me.

Have you ever found yourself pouting and whining about the very thing that God wants to use to make your life more in tune with him? Sometimes demanding our own way and our own rights is how we act out. Living up means submitting to God in our circumstances. Oswald Chambers speaks about interruptions shaping us:

> A saint's life is in the hands of God like a bow and arrow in the hands of an archer. God is aiming at something the saint cannot see, but our Lord continues to stretch and strain, and every once in a while the saint says, "I can't take any more." Yet God pays no attention: He goes on stretching until His purpose is in sight, and then He lets the arrow fly. Entrust yourself to God's hands.[1]

We can either try to develop ourselves—which doesn't seem to work for long—or we can embrace the wilder development process and allow God to have his way with us. Neither are "fun" in the moment, but yielding to God's shaping process is definitely more productive than trying to whip ourselves into shape. I wish that being wild was about having more fun. Like most, I am familiar with the American lifestyle of instant gratification. Girls just want to have fun, right? But I will tell you a secret. Growing in Christ is beyond fun, because there is nothing quite like realizing that God is actually changing you—for real. Real life change is exciting, almost intoxicating. And when you recognize it's God's Spirit at work in you, your faith in Christ grows to a whole new level.

My friend Nora has been changing at a steady pace this year. After years of being a Christian who tried with all her might to get it "right" on her own, Nora gave up and surrendered it all to Jesus. She had done this many times before, but this time the difference was a growing intimacy that was taking her to a deeper place than she had ever been. This time her decision to surrender came by learning to follow Christ, as simplistic as that seems, even in the hard situations. I guess you can say she was learning, in real-life ways, how to live up.

Nora works at a prestigious retail store as a commissioned salesperson. With the economy down, so were sales and employee morale. But even in a down economy, Nora trusted that God would be her family's provision. With just enough gas in her tank for the week and just enough food for a few days, she was content in knowing God kept providing.

One Friday morning she had the perfect opportunity to act out. While Nora was helping a customer who had gone into the fitting room, her co-worker came up and slapped her, accusing Nora of stealing the customer from her. At the sting of the slap on her arm, Nora had a wild thought: *Jesus, what would you have me do right now? Jesus, I know I belong to you. Show me how to respond to this.*

She decided to try something "different." Nora didn't act out. Instead, she kept her cool, continued helping the customer when she came out of the dressing room, and dealt with the angry co-worker later. And how did she deal with her?

Nora went and found Charlene in the break room and began to talk to her. "I am not sure what that was all about, but it wasn't okay to slap me," she said. "I know times are hard and we are all struggling. I would like to give you half of my commission on that sale. The customer ended up spending over three thousand dollars, and God always provides what I need, so I want to help you out."

A stunned Charlene was embarrassed and speechless. Nora gave her an affectionate pat and went on her way, joy abounding and a spring in her step. But it didn't end there.

The whole incident was recorded by store security on hidden camera. The next day the human resources department called Nora in and asked her to press charges. She was assured that hitting another employee was against company policy and that Charlene would be let go. Nora began explaining to the human resources supervisor how terrible that would be.

"Charlene is a single parent. She is struggling. I do not want to press charges. I handled it already."

"How did you handle it?"

"I told her it wasn't cool to do that to me, and then I gave her half of my commission."

"What? Why would you do that?"

"I wanted to bless her. God always provides for me, and my heart went out to her. She must really be hurting to act out the way she did."

Well, news quickly got back to Charlene about Nora refusing to press charges or file a report with the HR department. Charlene could not believe it and began opening up to Nora and allowing Nora to share Christ and the hope she had with her. The story had a happy ending: at the time of this writing three of Nora's non-Christian co-workers, including Charlene, have decided to join her at church. Why? Her faith was real, not tamed or silenced. What began as an ordinary day in May turned into an extraordinary one. Nora became a wild example of a woman who trusted God with her own outcome and lived to love others in the process.

And the fun part? Jesus changed Nora and she knew it. You see, she had a background that no one knew about. A few years earlier her own children were taken out of her home because she was accused of physical abuse and having anger issues. How could it be that someone with an underlying issue with anger could change so much that she turned the other cheek in the heat of the moment? Wild, isn't it? Proof once again that Jesus changes people, developing them and making them different when they surrender all to him. Nora began soaring after that experience.

Development Is a Slow Process

Sitting on the table next to me is a magazine, the cover of which promises I will find 122 quick changes for health, body, home, and happiness. I must admit, I am a sucker for this stuff. It also promises that I can lose thirty pounds without even trying and redo any room in the house in just forty-eight hours. But the most alluring promise for me is that I can look five years younger fast—and with no surgery!

I like promises. Promises offer hope and possibility. Unfortunately, all the promises for quick fixes end up leaving me more hopeless than hopeful—because they draw me in and then suck me dry when I don't perform well enough to get the prize. Sometimes life seems like a lot of promises that never get fulfilled or a bunch of dreams that we never really get to live. "If only I could be . . ." (fill in your desire of the day or hour). This longing to "arrive" plagues us, drives us, and keeps us from enjoying the moments that make up a day—and the days that make up a life. We miss out on the beauty of life in the moment when we are chronically trying to fix ourselves.

God has a different promise:

> The LORD will fulfill his purpose for me;
> your love, O LORD, endures forever—
> do not abandon the works of your hands.
>
> Psalm 138:8

I made a wild decision some time ago to step off the wheel of perfection and find the peace that awaits me when I trust my "stuff" to the God who loves me. It's wild to stop the insanity of trying to be perfect. It's off the normal course of female behavior, isn't it? It's wilder still to welcome the slow process of development, finding peace there.

Slow is not popular these days. Speed is sexy, speed is acceptable, speed is strong—but speed is not usually how God works his ways in us.

If you have done much Bible reading, you have probably noted that Jesus told his disciples that they were to be perfect: "Be perfect, therefore, as your heavenly Father is perfect" (Matt. 5:48). Maybe you have taken that "perfect" word and run with it.

The word *perfect* here is not the perfect that we are accustomed to. It is from the Greek work *teleios*, which means mature and finished. When the Bible speaks of aiming for perfection, it is telling us to aim for maturity. This maturity translates into being made complete, changed into what we were made to be. This is worlds apart from the kind of perfect women try to achieve today.

Paul even tells us that the way to achieve maturity and strength is through our weaknesses. God told him, "My grace is sufficient for you, for My strength is made perfect [mature, finished, complete] in weakness" (2 Cor. 12:9 NKJV). We live in a world that applauds strength. As Christians we serve a God who uses our weaknesses and pain to bring us into true strength. This is not the world's plan for strength building, but it is God's, and it is good news.

Turning our mind-set around is going to be a wild thing. It's going to be different from the cultural norm. But that is what wild is—a different life.

Oswald Chambers says, "We are not meant to be seen as God's perfect, bright-shining examples, but to be seen as the everyday essence of ordinary life exhibiting the miracle of His grace."[2]

The focus of life was never meant to be on getting ourselves together. Self-focus robs us of spiritual focus. This skewed focus is a giant distraction from the peace of relationship that we can have in Christ. In Christ, we were meant to find freedom from the pressure of being "better." Trusting ourselves to his process in our lives is a new way to live.

Lesson in a Drawer

One day not long ago while looking for something important, I happened upon several loose rolls of used film rolling around the bottom of a messy catch-all drawer. Though these rolls of film were not what I was looking for that day, the sight of them made my mind go places I hadn't expected to go. *"I wonder how old these rolls of film are? Whose faces or what places will I see when these are developed? What has been forgotten that will be found?"*

I snatched up the film and put it somewhere where it wouldn't be overlooked again. The next day I dropped off the film for processing. What happened next is where the beauty begins—because before I ever got the end result, those glossy prints in my hands, the film had to go through a process. The same is true with us.

We are all in a process of development. Many things shape us throughout the course of our lives. Often we aren't even aware of the impact, but God knows exactly where he is taking us and what he is bringing to life within us through each circumstance.

My mother's last words to me were, "Live like it's real—because it is." Her words, spoken about what she was experiencing at death, were a charge to me and my children for how to live our lives on earth. It's been ten years since I heard her voice, and for ten years I have internally been hearing the call to live differently—intentionally differently.

The moment I heard her words, I believed I was in a holy moment, a moment in time when God was making himself more real to me than ever before. And through the past ten years, God has continued to call me closer to himself and further away from me as I knew me. That girl who wanted her way and only her way has submitted to the rule of God, and now I want only to be wildly surrendered to the God who created me. I certainly fall short, but I have peace in knowing I am firmly in the processing solution of God's Spirit. I'm like the roll of film—dropped in the bin and being developed.

Film was made to capture images, but in order to do what it was made for, it has to be developed. And as simplistic as it sounds, in order for us to experience the life God has called us to live, we too must be developed. For us, development is a lifelong process. We don't get to drop our little hearts in a bin and pick them up the next day fully developed, glossy, beautiful, and ready for framing. With film, yes—but not with real lives. In reality growth is a lifelong process of development. It's becoming all that God has designed for us to become—individually—as his women.

Development might be a new thought for some of us. We are familiar with striving to arrive at a goal, but development? Development is very different from perfection or arriving—development is a process. Striving for perfection creates an atmosphere of being driven to be better, while embracing the idea of process gives us the freedom to be shaped and changed in God's timing. The dictionary defines *develop* as:

- to realize the possibilities of
- to grow or expand gradually
- to make more available or more effective
- to enlarge, to process
- to make the latent image visible
- to progress in stages of maturity

How do those definitions relate to your own spiritual growth as a woman? It's actually exciting to realize that when God is developing us, a lot of very good things are going on. The end result is to expand us, to enlarge our heart and make himself more visible in us. When we are developing, we are making progress. During development we are growing, becoming more effective, and becoming more available to God's work in and through us.

Development over perfection?

Process over perfection?

Now that's a thought. Look at the definitions of these two very different ways to live—process versus perfection.

process: a series of steps toward a desired end; a natural gradual change from one state to another; to prepare, convert, make useable

perfection: the state or quality of being
perfect (without defect or fault)

Unfortunately, we live in a world that applauds achievement so much that many base their entire identity on the approval of others or the glow of accomplishment. In reality it is not God's dream to make us perfect women. God's dream is that we learn to find joy in the process of living in him. When we live in his development plan, our lives take on a new shape one step at a time.

The Process Brings Beauty to Life

A few days after I dropped it off undeveloped, I picked up my processed film. The development process yielded beautiful four-by-six-inch color photos. As I looked at each picture, I experienced the full potential of the film that was once just stuck in the bottom of my drawer.

After being developed, the once unprocessed film became a new adventure for me to enjoy. It was after the process that I could see the beauty of smiling faces and familiar places. As film goes through the developing process, colors pop, images emerge, and we see life captured in full color. As I held those pictures in my hands, I was also reminded that God works in much the same way as he is developing me. Like a treasure hunt, life is all about the process.

Perfectionism leads to dissatisfaction and discontentment, while process leads to the beginning of experiencing abundant life. It's a good start to recognize perfection as a trap, but in order to embrace process over perfection, we need to understand God's development plan a little more. Getting a grip on this process of development is the next step in finding freedom to truly live beyond ourselves.

In Romans 8:28 we see that God is working all things together for our good, but in verse 29 we see another part of the process that God wants us to understand: "For whom He foreknew, He also predestined to be conformed into the image of His Son" (NKJV). Or as Eugene Peterson puts it in *The Message*, "God knew what he was doing from the very beginning. He decided from the outset to shape the lives of those who love him along the same lines as the life of his Son."

Living in the Developing Solution of God's Purpose

God's purpose is to shape us into his image—that is the purpose of the process of development. Process breeds maturity, which Webster's says is "having achieved full growth or development." Sounds like that Greek word *teleios*, doesn't it?

Growing up spiritually might scare some of us. Like children, we want what we want, when we want it. As grown-up girls, our toys are different from when we were two years old, but we still like to pout, disobey, and demand our way.

Insisting on having our way, our rights, and our plans is childish, immature, and unspiritual—it's also our American normal. That is why moving against that norm is so wild. It's wild to be standing for something or in something that is not the acceptable norm. Becoming this kind of wild has become my goal for myself and for many of the women I know.

This doesn't happen with a spiritual to-do list or a perfectly put together life plan. It happens when life happens and we embrace the process of spiritual development. Once embraced, the process of maturity can develop us, expand us, and forever change us. It's like living outside the perfection box—because in development we are in the process of becoming, rather than the mad dash of trying to arrive.

Signing Our Name on the Processing Envelope

God has a plan to develop us. But as with my rolls of film, something has to happen to get us from point A to point B. I had to take the film to the processing center, fill out the proper form, and drop the envelope into the bin. We have to sign up for the processing by saying yes to God and then dropping our life into his hands, allowing him to do his gradual work in us—a work that takes a lifetime. And just as we see in the dictionary definition of what it means to develop something, God then takes our lives and makes the image of Christ in us begin to come forth a little more each day. Only when we say yes to the process do we begin to realize the possibilities of what God has created us for in the first place.

I didn't plan to end up in a wheelchair that spring day two years ago. I had a hard time with the physical rehabilitation, the pain, and the boredom of my life being interrupted. But I learned once again that embracing the process is the only way to get through to the other end with my spiritual senses intact.

I can get through to the other side screaming and yelling, or I can get through to the other side looking for God in the process. Either way, I will go through things in life, and my life will not be perfect. I get to choose to embrace the plan of God to develop me—a wild choice. Or I can rebel against everything that he is doing and spend my days acting out.

We all get to choose. The rest of this book will spell out how to walk in new choices.

Wild women choose to embrace the process because they understand they are not of this world. I was asked to follow God from a wheelchair for a season. Where are you today? And how is he asking you to follow him?

Christian perfection is not, and never can be, human perfection. Christian perfection is the perfection of a relationship with God that shows itself to be true even amid the seemingly unimportant aspects of human life.

Oswald Chambers

Wild Strategies for Living in Process, Not Perfection

Look Up

- What does God value?
- God created you and knows all the potential waiting inside of you. Thank him for knowing every cell, every creative gift, every plan to use your life.
- Thank him today that he created you as his roll of film with images to capture, purposes to fulfill.

Pray Up

- Ask for a mind-set of development and contentment in being in his developing solution.
- Ask, seek, and knock—bring everything you think of to God during all your processes.

Live Up

- Turn away from the worthless task of trying to perfect yourself in your own strength, and don't allow anyone to pull you into that carnal trap again.
- Choose to trust God with the potential that has been placed in you and his power to call it forth.
- Walk in truth as proclaimed in Scripture and turn away from the lies that are prevalent in our culture.

Questions for Reflection on the Wild Life

1. How has perfectionism affected you?
2. Do you ever feel pressure to "get yourself together"?

3. If so, how do you generally go about accomplishing that?
4. Read Ephesians 2:1–3 and think about your life up to this point.
5. Are you currently conforming more to this world or living in a wildly different reality than what is culturally acceptable as the norm?

4

Wild Women
Follow after God

> The Christian is a person who recognizes that our real problem is not in achieving freedom but in learning service under a better master. . . . We urgently want to live under the mastery of God.
>
> Eugene Peterson[1]

*W*omen who follow after God are passionate, free, unconventional, and courageous. These wild traits don't pop up overnight, but they take root over time as we walk through real life, following hard after a better master—God.

Anne desperately wanted to follow after God and longed to do so consistently. She was growing in an intimacy with her heavenly Father that she never dreamed could be possible. She was also in the home stretch of raising her son Eric. His

six-foot frame was proof that he had grown up, but as graduation day neared, her heartstrings tugged repeatedly as she was
reminded many times that this boy, the one who was getting
ready to go off to college, was once her baby. Nostalgia set
in, and daily tears became Anne's norm.

Anne was distraught because her ex-husband and his new
live-in girlfriend were planning to be at the ceremony, posing
as the original family. She felt insulted and angry. She was
afraid of how she might react. So she had no intention on
giving one of those hard-to-come-by graduation tickets to
her ex for his girlfriend. No way. She was the mom. No new
live-in girlfriend was going to be smiling at the camera with
her son, and no other woman was going to fix his cap and
gown—no other woman was going to even begin to think
she could ever stand in as Eric's mom.

So Anne set out to control how everything would play out.
Until . . . that still small voice—often attributed to God—
began to change her direction. Suddenly she knew what she
didn't want to know and heard what she didn't want to hear.
God was asking her for something she didn't want to give:
the ticket.

As she recounted her inner dialogue with me, I heard her
pain and also heard how God was nudging that tender heart
of hers—and how she was learning to hear him and desiring
to respond to his way. Her internal struggle went something
like, *But God, you've got to be kidding. You can't be asking
me to go along with this. I am the mother, and she . . . she . . .
that woman, that home wrecker, that non-mother, has even
put her picture in Eric's yearbook wishing him well—like she
is his mother. She is not his mother—I am! She can't come
to graduation. All the attention will be on her—the other
woman—in her short miniskirt and low-cut top. We should all
be focused on Eric, but with her there, all eyes will be on her.
I cannot bear this, Lord. Surely you understand. Don't you?*

God met Anne right where she was, and he seemed to be
saying, *Yes . . . I do understand. But this really isn't about Eric,*

is it? It's more about you. You are far more worried about you being able to handle things than whether it will be good for Eric to have her there. He probably would like her to attend. She is, for better or worse, in his father's life. You cannot change what has happened. I know that if you do give her the ticket, pushing through the ugliness of the situation, you will finally begin to be healed, and you will be on the road to finding freedom. You have held on for far too long. You cannot change people; only I can do that. I can change you, you know. Follow me, and I will change you. I know you, remember? I know everything about you, and I am set on healing you. Follow me. I will protect you. Follow me. I will use everything that you walk through. Follow me.

Anne listened and followed. Though it is hard to follow when it requires doing something we don't want to do, it is usually these moments of following God that become the most precious memories of God's faithfulness and personal growth.

Come and Follow

There is a wild principle here for women who are ready to live wild. Jesus said it thousands of years ago to two fishermen, and he says it again to us today in our here and now: "Follow me" (Matt. 4:19). There you have it. Those two words spell out an important step in the Christian journey. Jesus calls us to *come*, which means to move toward, and then he tells us to *follow*.

Following Jesus is simple in wording but not simple in action. Giving up the lead of our life to someone else, even God, is a bit, well . . . unnerving. That is, until we understand the promise that is attached to the call to follow.

The most important aspect of following is letting go. To follow another, we must let go of our path and trust their direction. As Kitty Crenshaw and Catherine Snapp write:

Trust and letting go work mysteriously together. Nothing ever stays the same in our lives, and again and again, we are called to let go in order to find a new way. If we continue to cling to the past and never dare to let go, we will never learn to trust. Our choice is this: to become more bound up trying to fight the reality we find ourselves in and hold on to our own illusion of control, or to become more free by trusting God's goodness and desire to move us to a new place of freedom. The more we believe God truly loves us and wants what is best for us, the easier it becomes to believe that everything that is happening is exactly as it should be.[2]

Jesus always approached people with the message of letting go of where they were at and taking hold of the promise that he was the Messiah and could change them, heal them, forgive them, and bring something different to their lives. Take a look at the account of when Jesus began his ministry:

> As Jesus was walking beside the Sea of Galilee, he saw two brothers, Simon called Peter and his brother Andrew. They were casting a net into the lake, for they were fishermen. "Come, follow me," Jesus said, "and I will make you fishers of men." At once they left their nets and followed him.
>
> Matthew 4:18–19

Now, if you have been around Christian circles for long, this story is familiar to you. Perhaps you're experiencing a ho-hum attitude right now. But stretch with me here, and look at the deeper meaning in what Jesus was doing, what he was saying, and how it relates to us today. Sure, we see that he asked them to follow; we have all heard that before. And we may have also heard that they immediately put down their nets and followed. All good things to know. But do you see the beauty of the promise in what Jesus was offering them?

Jesus told them that if they followed, he would make them something different. Did you hear that? Let me say it again, relating it to us today: Jesus said if we follow him, he will make us someone different!

Rather than fishing for fish, they would fish for people. In other words, they would be changed, and the outcome of their lives would be changed too. Oh, this is so amazing! I don't know about you, but I want to be something different. I want a different outcome and a life that is an expression of Christ. I want to live in the context of a faith that is beyond myself. Wanting something different is probably why I am such a sucker for the magazine covers that promise me wealth in retirement and a flatter belly. So understanding this first step is not only foundational; it could very well be earth shattering if we dared to try following—and then dared to believe God is the difference maker in our lives.

Jesus changes us and makes our lives something different when we follow. What does it mean to follow?

- to come or go after
- to chase or pursue
- to accompany or journey with
- to comply with or obey
- to pay attention to

For some of us, the idea of following Jesus simply means going to church. That might be a good start, but it isn't really what following Jesus is. Truth is, you can actually follow Jesus without a church building. To follow Jesus is personal, intimate, and sometimes private. To follow after God is to journey with him through life, pursuing a relationship with him, paying attention to his directions, and obeying his lead.

Maybe this is the key to change for some of us. I encourage you to ask yourself the question "Have I followed?" I am not asking if you have gone to church or signed up to help with the next activity. And I'm not asking if you have changed your ways from being a club hopper to being a church girl. The question is much more than that. Have you laid down your net and begun to follow fast and hard after God?

Following Good Ideas or Following God?

I will give you a true confession here: most of my Christian walk has been spent following good God ideas, not following God. Because of this, I have spent significant time spinning my wheels and not realizing much difference or life change. But the truth is, Jesus Christ came to redeem us from ourselves and to be the difference maker in our lives. If we follow him, he promises, he will change us. Period.

Jesus didn't ask the fishermen to create new nets. He simply said lay them down, and if you will, when you follow me you will be more fruitful and more effective. Ken Gire speaks of following after God as joining him in the dance:

> He doesn't ask us to write the notes to the music or choreograph the steps to the dance. He asks us merely to take his hand and follow him. To move when he moves. To speed up when he speeds up. To slow down when he slows down. And to stop when he stops.[3]

If you want to get real here, it's unbelievable that he has even picked us and asked us to dance. More unbelievable is that when we dance with him, following his lead, we are transformed and changed into more than we could be all by ourselves.

Dependent and Afraid

As I worked through my feelings about being totally dependent on my family after my leg injury, I began to see how much my independence had kept me from being close to God and depending on him. I had become accustomed to doing things in my own strength. Without my own strength, I was afraid. I felt small, insecure, and yes, insignificant.

I could not do all that I had been used to doing. But in that wheelchair I learned something very important: no matter where I was or how much I couldn't do, I could still learn to follow after God, because following after God has to start with the heart, not with the feet. I also began to realize that when I am in control, I often get things wrong and mess them up.

Anne was ready to mess things up too. Had she not given the extra ticket to her ex-husband, she most likely would have begun to alienate her own son. He had no problem understanding that his dad's girlfriend was not his mother. But this new woman had become Eric's friend, and as his friend and his father's significant other, she was someone Eric would want there with his dad. Anne was on a tightrope and didn't even know it at the time. Her self-focus, caused by emotional pain and fear, was blinding her from following the spiritual truth of living generously toward all people, letting go of offenses and past hurts, and loving others because of Christ's law of love.

To Chase and Pursue

In order for us to chase after God, pursuing his path, we have to lay down our own. That is what was happening with those fishermen. They began really living once they laid down their nets and followed after Jesus. They ended up seeing things they would have never seen if they had stayed on the lakeshore doing their own thing. They experienced God's power in ways they never would have had they not turned and followed. It makes me wonder how many things I have missed while insisting on my own agenda!

If Christ were to walk alongside you today, what net would he be asking you to lay down? Jesus died for us, laying down his life for our lives and freedom. We are called to lay down our lives and our nets and follow after him. It's not easy to lay down your life day after day. It is contrary to our human nature to lay down our lives, our desires, our dreams—for anyone. Most especially for a God we cannot see.

Oswald Chambers talks about this in *My Utmost for His Highest*:

> If I am a friend of Jesus, I must deliberately and carefully lay down my life for Him. It is a difficult thing to do, and thank God that it is. Salvation is easy for us, because it cost God so much. But the exhibiting of salvation in my life is difficult. God saves a person, fills him with the Holy Spirit, and then says, in effect, "Now you work it out in your life, and be faithful to Me, even though the nature of everything around you is to cause you to be unfaithful."[4]

That's why following is so wild—because everything around us urges us to follow our own hearts, our own dreams, our own selves, rather than following Jesus.

Living for Him

Obedience means living for Christ, paying attention to his voice, and following after that voice. If I do what is right, not for duty's sake but because I believe God is who he says he is, and that this big and mighty God is engineering my circumstances, then at the point of following him into obedience, all the grace of God is mine, working on my behalf and enabling me to come to him in a real way that changes my everyday moments.

Before Jesus called the disciples to ministry, he called them to intimacy. This is important to remember. We are conditioned to "do," but first God is calling us to "be." He is calling us to follow him in the pursuit of learning what it means to "be his."

For the disciples, following (being with him) came first, fishing (doing) came later. Before he called them to go out and represent him, he called them to be with him. Before he sent them out, he drew them close. This same Jesus wants to draw us close today too. But we get it backward, don't we? It is natural for us to set out to do things for God, in his name—things earmarked with kingdom purpose. It's easier for us to say yes to being on a church or community committee than it is to truly say yes to seeking the heart of God. Too bad that it isn't as natural for us to be with him in thought, in frequent prayer, in looking up for heaven's perspective, in praying up for heaven's answers, and in living up for heaven's action. The point is, it starts with being with him, then becomes doing for him—not the other way around.

We get so caught up in doing life "right" and finding steps to success that we forget about the essential love of God for us. It is a love so all-encompassing that it caused Paul to say, "The love of God compels me, so that I no longer live for myself, but for him" (see 2 Cor. 5:14–15). Luke tells us that the credentials by which the disciples were recognized were not influential or normal worldly credentials; instead, the disciples were known as those who "had been with Jesus" (Acts 4:13).

What credentials are you falling back on today? We follow our credentials, don't we? If you are a doctor, you follow that path. If you are a musician, you follow that path. If you are a mother, you follow that path. But what if in the midst of our worldly titles and credentials, there is an underlying credential that would support them all?

Being with Jesus each day is something different and something wild. It causes us to be passionately enthusiastic. It makes us energized enough spiritually to lay down our nets, listen to his voice, and look for his power and supply.

As in anything else, we each have a choice: to love or not to love. To dance or not to dance. To follow or not to follow. To give up the ticket to graduation as a response to God's voice or to hold on with clenched fists to our own rights and attitudes.

But in the end, it's only when we lay down our lives and follow him that we become different. Jesus said that the single most important thing was to love him with all of who we are (see Matt. 22:37). The word for love here is *agapao*, and it does not refer to an emotional feeling or response. It is a love of choice. To love God (*agapao* him) is to lay down our lives, surrender our will, and learn to live in a moment-by-moment relationship—a constant surrender of our total being. This is intimacy with the Father: allowing him total access to every part of us—heart, soul, strength, and mind. And, though this is not going to sound socially correct, to love God is really to lose oneself.

Wild? Yes! A bit scary? Yes, it can be. Totally freeing? Absolutely. In this place we can experience Christ living in and through us. Remember the wild prayer: "Less of me and more of thee." As we decrease and he increases, great things begin to take shape in our lives. Wild things. Contrary things. Things out of the ordinary. When he increases, our life is filled up with faith moments.

All my life I have been longing for something different. And now I get it—Jesus is the difference maker in my midst. Jesus is waiting for me to heed the call and make the choice to follow. Jesus is calling me to the wild life of faith, the life I was born to live and experience. Jesus is calling me to the dance of love.

> It's fine and politically correct to believe in God, but to really love Him is a whole different story.
>
> Chris Tomlin[5]

71

And what about you?

What do you hear Jesus speaking to your heart right now?

What net do you need to lay down?

What music calls you out to the dance floor?

Who will be the leading man in your life?

Wild Strategies for Following after Jesus

Look Up

- You can't follow toward heaven when your gaze is earthbound. Determine to look up and stand tall as you follow after God each day. Slip into your "God shoes" and stand firm in faith. We can't see the things we hope for; that is what faith is—hoping with assurance that God will provide all we need. If we follow, he will make the difference.

Pray Up

- He wants to hear your voice, your prayer, your request—make all known to him.
- Lay every stray thought and emotion at his feet.
- Afraid to follow? Tell him so. Afraid to obey his direction? Let him know. Pray for the strength to make the right choices in obedience.

Live Up

- Life is lived in the moments that make up a day. Live moment by moment with the thought of his presence, his power, and his love.
- What is he pressing into your heart? How is he nudging you today? Respond to that still small voice by saying yes to whatever he is asking of you.

Questions for Reflection on the Wild Life

1. Read Matthew 4:18–19, picturing the scene and what was taking place.
2. Jesus asked them to follow. What does that mean to you today?
3. One of the meanings of "follow" is to pay attention to. Are you skilled at paying attention to the Lord's voice?
4. What has God been speaking to you that might be hard to understand or hard to follow?
5. Read Acts 4:13. What is this saying to you today? Have you hung out with Jesus lately?

Part

Two

Daring

Living by a Different Standard

Live as free men, but do not use your freedom
as a cover-up for evil; live as servants of God.

1 Peter 2:16

The presence of vanity, egotism, hostility,
fear, indifference, and downright meanness
can be counted among professing Christians.
The opposite of those qualities—the fruit of
the Spirit—cannot be simply assumed in the
typical Christian group.

Dallas Willard[1]

5

Wild Women Choose
to Love Others

> If I have a faith that can move mountains, but
> have not love, I am nothing.
>
> 1 Corinthians 13:2

*E*ach day we make choices. We decide what we will wear, where we will go, and the companions we will go with. We also choose each day whom we will serve. Will we follow and serve Christ? Or will we follow ourselves and serve the self-life or habits of our flesh?

Marilyn was beside herself. Her two sisters were ganging up on her, and a family feud had broken out. Not understanding what this was really all about, Marilyn kept trying to get to the bottom of the drama. Finally, frustrated and "done," she set out to separate herself from their hurt and the lies that they were tangled up in as a family. But God had other plans for Marilyn.

It was time for faith to take a front seat and love to guide her life. Marilyn's natural tendency was to deflect and become defensive. After all, she had every right to be upset and angry at her sisters—they had done her wrong. Laying her head on her desk, she began to cry out to God, "Lord, I already know how to act out in this situation—in fact, I am good at it. I know how to hurt back and strike while the iron is hot. But I don't want to act out anymore. I want to live up. Jesus, show me what living up looks like in this picture."

Almost as soon as the amen left her lips, a verse popped into her mind. "As far as it depends on you, live at peace with everyone" (Rom. 12:18). She thought, *Live at peace with my sisters? Really? They have been so hateful and hurtful. They should be running to me with apologies for all they have done.* Again the verse ran through her mind and into her heart: "As much as it depends on you, live at peace with all men." *Depends on me? What depends on me?* Marilyn's mind raced, looking for any loophole in the situation. She didn't want to take any responsibility; it was much easier to blame others.

Before long she picked up the phone and asked her sisters to meet with her. She sat and humbly asked them to forgive her if she had done anything to offend them—although, remember, they had done the offending. She expressed her love for them.

Naturally they were stubborn at first, but love disarmed the enemy in their midst. Before long the three sisters were reunited, and it would not have happened unless one of them had heeded the call to the wild love that the Bible speaks of.

Love is not optional for you as God's Woman in Lifelong Development. Love is a key part of the lifestyle that we are being shaped into. Because God is love (love is the nature of who he is), following after him and becoming increasingly more like him requires following after love. Remember, when a Pharisee asked Christ what the most important commandment was, he replied with one theme—love.

"Love the Lord your God with all your heart and with all your soul and with all your mind." This is the first and greatest commandment. And the second is like it: "Love your neighbor as yourself." All the Law and the Prophets hang on these two commandments.

Matthew 22:37–40

In keeping with this theme of the Christian life, the apostle Paul said, "If I speak in the tongues of men and of angels, but have not love, I am only a resounding gong or a clanging cymbal. . . . If I have a faith that can move mountains, but have not love, I am nothing. If I give all I possess to the poor and surrender my body to the flames, but have not love, I gain nothing" (1 Cor. 13:1–3). He even referred to love as the greatest of gifts and the most excellent way (see 1 Cor. 12:31). I guess we can conclude that love is an important and pivotal part of following Jesus.

We Have a Problem

When it comes to love, we have a problem. And though it's hard to admit, more times than not, we are the problem. Why? Because we can be selfish and unloving. We can have manners on the outside but madness on the inside. We usually want our rights and our way. All of this deferring to "self" stands in the way of loving as Christ did. If the problem is us, then it's time we take a look at what it is in us that needs to be submitted to God. This submission is the wild life. Hold on because God's love, his unconditional love, will take you places you have never been.

We begin by admitting our inadequacy to carry out the command to love in our own effort, strength, or human reasoning. Let's be real here: Christians don't love automatically. We have our own hurts and insecurities that get played out in our relationships with other people. Unfortunately, deciding to follow Jesus doesn't automatically flip on a love switch.

It's easy to think that love should flow out of our every pore once we have committed our lives to Christ. When we don't overflow with love, we get confused and filled with personal shame. We think that maybe we aren't "good enough" Christians, and we try harder. News flash—there is no such thing as a "good enough" Christian:

> There is no one righteous, not even one.
>
> Romans 3:10

We are not "good enough," not one of us. But Christ, in his love, is our solution:

> For all have sinned and fall short of the glory of God, and are justified freely by his grace through the redemption that came by Christ Jesus.
>
> Romans 3:23–24

> Not that we are competent in ourselves to claim anything for ourselves, but our competence comes from God. He has made us competent as ministers of a new covenant—not of the letter but of the Spirit; for the letter kills, but the Spirit gives life.
>
> 2 Corinthians 3:5–6

As long as our goal is to be "good enough," we will always be missing out on living in the Truth that only God is good and it's enough that he lives in us.

Living by Faith

We come to Christ as women of human flesh, and as we surrender our lives to his will, things begin to change. Christ is good enough, and we now stand in his goodness. That is what taking a walk on the wild side is all about. It's not enough to know you are in Christ; now is the time to *stand* in him—and it always begins and ends with love. But just as spiritual growth doesn't happen overnight, so learning to love and relate to other people God's way is a process of growth and surrender.

Loving God's way starts with recognizing that God's love is different from human love. We do not need to learn techniques for how to love like God. We cannot learn to do what only God can do. Instead, we need to learn what it means to yield to the Holy Spirit of love within us, so that Christ's life and love can flow out from us.

In order for us to do this, we must:

- recognize the importance of yielding ourselves daily to God;
- realize that we have to choose to set aside our own emotions and desires that are contrary to God's, so that he can then love through us;
- remember that we can't change our pasts, we can't change other people, and we can't change circumstances where others' choices are involved.

Though we can't change some things, we can keep our eyes focused on Jesus, yield ourselves totally to him each day, and allow his love to flood our souls and overflow into all of our relationships and experiences. It all begins with relationship—first with God and then with others.

The Case of the Wrong Bags

On a speaking trip several months ago, I picked up a little suitcase off the luggage carousel. It looked like mine. But when I got to my hotel and opened the bag, I found a nice business suit, a bright flashy tie, and some men's boxers. It definitely was not my bag! Now I had a choice: either wear this size 44 suit to speak that night or get to the airport to make the exchange. I don't look good in size 44 men's suits and couldn't stand the look of that flashy tie, so my choice was easy.

If only it were so easy to decide to swap our personal baggage for God's love and grace. But if we don't make the exchange, we will forever be living by our own means, as carnal people, rather than by God's power as the spiritual people, the royal priesthood, that Scripture says we are. Remember, we were born of flesh and blood and reborn of the Spirit. One nature came wired for living according to the flesh (what Scripture refers to as our carnal nature), and the other released us to live instead in the power of the Spirit. We no longer have to live by our flesh and carnal human nature. We can instead choose to keep in step with the Spirit within us by yielding our wills, emotions, and choices to God and his power. I think of this as occurring in three parts:

1. We begin by recognizing the flesh nature within us.
2. Then we repent of our desire to follow it (to repent simply means to turn away from).
3. Finally, we turn toward the Spirit response (this is opposite of our flesh response) and move in that direction. This new direction is only possible because we have been born of the Spirit, made new in Christ, and given a new identity as his.

Living in our new identity does not have to do with us trying harder; it has everything to do with Christ being alive in us, working and touching others through us. Being wild isn't about a set of rules. Being wild is a matter of the heart—a matter of relationship over religion. Love of any kind begins with relationship.

Max Lucado speaks of the importance of relationship:

Certain things no one can do for you. You don't say, "I'm in love with that wonderful person, but romance is such a hassle.

I'm going to hire a surrogate lover to enjoy the romance in my place. I'll hear about it and be spared the inconvenience." Who would do that? Perish the thought. You want the romance firsthand. You don't want to miss a word or a date, and you certainly don't want to miss the kiss, right? Certain things no one can do for you.[1]

There is a difference between religion and relationship. If you are going to spend your life being religious, you will never be able to experience the wild ride of having God's love flow through you. Religion is a belief in a supernatural power—the head knowledge of spiritual things. Relationship is the connection between our spirit and the supernatural power. Relationship makes way for the life-flow of God's Spirit through us. It is possible to be religious without having relationship. We see this religion versus relationship example with the Pharisees. Jesus said to them:

> Woe to you, teachers of the law and Pharisees, you hypocrites! You are like whitewashed tombs, which look beautiful on the outside but on the inside are full of dead men's bones and everything unclean. In the same way, on the outside you appear to people as righteous but on the inside you are full of hypocrisy and wickedness.
>
> Matthew 23:27–28

Becoming a wild woman means moving beyond that kind of surface obedience. Being wild is not about fulfilling the externals. Wild living is walking in the power that enables us to go beyond ourselves.

We have a hard time understanding unconditional love. Examples of conditional love surround us. You scratch my back and I'll scratch yours. You give to me and I will give to you. But, don't think of crossing me, because then the love will be gone. Frances Chan speaks of this:

God wants to change us; He died so that we could change. The answer lies in letting Him change you. Remember His counsel to the lukewarm church in Laodicea?

> "Here I am! I stand at the door and knock. If anyone hears my voice and opens the door, I will come in and eat with him, and he with me."
>
> Revelation 3:20

His counsel wasn't to "try harder," but rather to let Him in.[2]

What is packed in your emotional luggage today? Anger, deep hurt, fears, bitterness, unforgiveness? Maybe you have religion packed in your bag, or the world's standards and philosophies. God will deal with us on those issues over time, but the first thing he wants us to unpack and exchange is religion. We must trade religion for the embrace of relationship.

What's Love Got to Do with It?

Magazine covers overflow with the promise of love—how to find it, how to keep it alive, and how to make it last. The Beatles sang "All You Need Is Love." And finding love has become the pursuit that is supposed to heal our hearts and fill every ache within us. The love we read about and hear about in the media is human love. We are born with it. Human love is the most beautiful flower the world has to offer, but it can hide a thorn, because it often causes heartaches, divorces, broken homes, and wrecked relationships.

Nancy Missler describes human love by saying:

- Human love is conditional because it depends on us— how we feel, what our circumstances are, or how the other person responds to us.
- Human love is bondage because it puts the one loving in bondage to expectations and forces the one being loved to respond from defenses rather than the heart.

- Human love is a self-centered love because it puts its own interests above the interests of others.[3]

There are three basic types of human love:

1. Storge love—*Storge* is the Greek word for our natural, emotional, or feeling love. Simply put, it is our affection love. It is instinctive love. *Storge* actually means "to cover over or to protect." It's the instinctive love of a parent for a child. Like all human or natural love, storge love can become a suffocating kind of love if the one being loved does not return it.
2. Eros love—*Eros* is the Greek word for our natural sexual love based on physical attraction. It is passionate, erotic love that has an intoxicating effect on us. One of the reasons we are so captivated by it is that it momentarily lifts us above ourselves. It is like a temporary escape. When eros love controls us, we will be carried on the tide of emotion. So without God's intervention, eros will always be a conditional love.
3. Phileo love—*Phileo* is Greek for anything we are strongly attached to. It is based on similarity of outlook and interest. It is mutual friendship, companionship, sharing common interest. Phileo is often called brotherly love.

C. S. Lewis said, "Human love is always a need love, with self-centered motives. But God's love is always a gift love, with no strings attached."[4] And the apostle Paul said that there was a more excellent way—and he then went on to describe God's love.

Contrary to human love stands God's love. Not everyone has God's love. God's love is a gift. And to receive this gift we must ask Jesus Christ into our hearts. Then his love, which is greater than any human love, is "poured into our hearts," as the apostle Paul says:

God has poured out his love into our hearts by the Holy
Spirit, whom he has given us.

Romans 5:5

Let us love one another, for love comes from God. Everyone
who loves has been born of God and knows God. . . . God
is love.

1 John 4:7–8

God's unconditional love is not based on human understanding, human desire, human emotion, others' responses,
or the circumstances we are in. It is dependent on God, and
he never changes, so neither does his love. John tells us that
we are to *agape* (unconditionally love) one another, for *agape*
comes from God. Everyone who *agapes* has been born of
God and knows God. God is *agape*—God is love. Nancy
Missler says:

- God's love is one-sided because it doesn't have to be
  returned to be kept alive.
- God's love is freeing because it frees the lover from expectations, allowing love to flow from the heart, not the
  defenses.
- God's love is an other-centered love because it always
  puts others' interests above its own.[5]

As we can see, God's love is unconditional. The difference
is paramount. Human love is self-centered, because no matter how selfless it looks on the outside, we will always hope
to get something in return. Receiving Christ and having him
live within us is what makes Christianity so totally different
from all other world religions. Christianity is the only religion
where God himself (who is love) comes to live within the
believer. Christians then live out their faith in relationship to
the indwelling Spirit, rather than religion and rules.

The Bible defines agape love for us:

Love is patient, love is kind. It does not envy, it does not boast, it is not proud. It is not rude, it is not self-seeking, it is not easily angered, it keeps no record of wrongs. Love does not delight in evil but rejoices with the truth. It always protects, always trusts, always hopes, always perseveres. Love never fails.

1 Corinthians 13:4–8

Agape Is Different

God's love is supernatural and different from our human love. If we continue making resolutions to love and making lists to check off our love actions toward others, we will forever be frustrated. Just as a plant's fruit depends on its connection to the vine, the love within us depends on our daily connection to Christ.

Agape love involves a choice. *Agapao* is the action verb used in the Bible for walking in God's love. God does the loving, not us. All he requires from us is that we choose to allow his love to love through us. We allow God to use us as an open vessel through which he can pour his love.

In order to be filled with agape, we will have to unpack something else—we will have to unpack any rebellion against God's way. Rebellion means defiance toward authority. We must unpack this kind of attitude so we can love. Human love wants its own way, while God's love is selfless. In order to walk in God's love, we will have to lay down our rebellion toward unconditional love. We will also need to unpack human love to be able to open the gift of God's love.

How Do We Get Filled with Agape?

God's love involves our will. Unlike human love, agape does not depend on emotions, thoughts, or desires. To be filled with God's love, we must make a choice to submit to God and his Spirit within us. We must recognize that:

- God's love was given as a gift upon salvation,
- God's love is the fruit of the Holy Spirit,
- God's love is God himself living through us,
- God's love is not a "thing" to be conquered but a person to be connected to.

Remember, agape is not automatic. Agape is also not just being nice. Being nice to others is just a Band-Aid. To be wild in the authority of God's love, we need something more than a Band-Aid. We need to be filled with Christ.

Agape is a life-flow, a powerful manifestation of God's Spirit within us. We can justify some of our hurts, unforgiveness, and resentments if we use the world's standards. But by God's standards, these negative emotions quench God's Spirit within us and become sin when we nurture them and entertain them.

Remember what Jesus said: "You do not belong to the world, but I have chosen you out of the world" (John 15:19), and "They are not of the world, even as I am not of it. Sanctify them by the truth; your word is truth" (John 17:16–17).

Here is the wild challenge: agape love involves choice— "this is my command: Love each other" (John 15:17).

In other words, Jesus commands you to let the love of God (God's love, not merely your human love) flow through you to others. Christ was not modeling human love; he came to do the will of the Father and to be the love of God in human form. As women in spiritual development, we take the action step of asking God to make us cleansed and available vessels of his love. We do this by connection and choice. The choice to connect and love is ours; the power to heal and deliver is God's.

Real freedom comes only with the experience and the practice of authentic love.

Eugenia Price[6]

Calling all wild women: "Let love be your highest goal" (1 Cor. 14:1 NLT).

As Christ develops his life in you, your life will take on these qualities: patience, kindness, no longer being envious of others, humility, no longer self-seeking, not easily angered, keeping no records when others do wrong, no longer delighting in evil but believing the best of others. You will begin protecting, trusting, hoping, persevering, and always staying faithful in the love walk (see 1 Cor. 13:4–7).

Remember, we are not perfect but rather in development. And as we develop, we will mature. We are in process. Oswald Chambers said, "It is the process, not the outcome that is glorifying to God."[7]

Wild living always requires following God—obeying his commands, principles, precepts, and plans. Making the choice to love is a step toward living up.

Are you ready to step out of your comfort zone?

Wild Strategies for Choosing God's Love

Look Up

- Find out what God says about his love.
- His love is different from any love we manufacture.

Pray Up

- Thank God that you have been filled with the love of God when it was poured into your heart as a gift at salvation.
- Thank him that in your own strength you cannot walk and live in that love.
- Ask God to forgive you for selfishness and wanting your own way.
- Ask him to fill you afresh daily with the love of Jesus.

Live Up

- Begin to move in who Jesus is, for God is love.
- Notice when you are living in a less-than-love place, and change directions.
- Step out of your comfort zone and reach out to people, because God loves people, and his love lives in you.

Questions for Reflection on the Wild Life

1. According to Matthew 22:37–40, what is the most important theme in this life?
2. Do you have things packed in your life luggage that keep you from experiencing the love of Christ flowing through you?
3. Do you generally live your life by faith or feelings? How did the Pharisees live?
4. Is love a feeling? A choice? A spiritual law? Or a combination?
5. Read John 15:17. What does this command mean to you today? How does it challenge you?

6

Wild Women Forgive
and Make Peace

If you judge people, you have no time to love
them.

Mother Teresa[1]

I didn't want to forgive—so I didn't. Instead, I walked
down the path of bitterness, resentment, and justified
hurt. This path was not a lonely one. In fact, many of the
people I trusted most were right alongside me. I cannot
count the times that I was encouraged to hold on to the
negative feelings I had for my ex-husband. After all, many
of my Christian friends verified that what he had done
was wrong and what I was doing was right. And most of
my friends, the ones I attended Bible studies with, were
entrenched in their own justified hurts and places of unforgiveness. I am ashamed to say that I held on tightly to

"justified" hurt for several years. I had no plan to forgive—instead, I put my ex into a little box and trusted that God was mad at him too. I was slowly being deceived and falling into the pit that Satan had dug for me—poisoned and polluted spiritually by choosing to believe unforgiveness was an option.

Forgiveness Is Not Optional

A walk on the wild side leads down a narrow road. Don't expect a crowd when you decide to make a stand and go against the conventional norm. It is different and wild to be a woman who follows Christ in the path of love and forgiveness. Quite frankly, I have found that it makes people uncomfortable. C. S. Lewis wrote, "Everyone says forgiveness is a lovely idea until they have something to forgive."[2] Jesus said:

> Enter through the narrow gate. For wide is the gate and broad is the road that leads to destruction, and many enter through it. But small is the gate and narrow the road that leads to life.
>
> Matthew 7:13–14

How do you usually respond when someone hurts you? Do you . . .

get angry	give the silent treatment	fume and fuss
become defensive	fight back	plot against the person
gossip	choose sides	get even/pay back
seek revenge	sulk	overeat/overdrink
get depressed	spin out emotionally	erect emotional walls

A wonderful counselor led me down the narrow road of learning the walk of God's agape love and forgiveness. I faced tough relationship choices. I had been hurt by divorce, hurt by Christians, and hurt by the cold reality of a life that didn't turn out the way I had planned. I was mad at the world.

Freedom in Christ

My inner turmoil led me to justify some very ugly actions that were certainly not appropriate for a Christian. I acted out in many fleshly ways during those days. I was overlooking my own sin while getting mad about my ex-husband's sin. It's safe to say that though no one could have convinced me at the time, I was off track—completely off track spiritually. I began to sink deeper and deeper into the pit of hate and despair. I was in agony. The more I hated, the worse my depression became. Then one day during my misery, my counselor looked me in the eye and said, "Debbie, I know you have been hurt, but your hurt will now carry on in your children if you do not give it to God. Do you want your children to have a legacy of hate, hurt, and bitterness? Or do you want to give them the legacy of love and forgiveness? You can't tell them about God's love if you aren't first walking in that love yourself."

Wise man. He knew how to get to me, because he knew I loved my children. Certainly I did not want to cause more damage in their lives, and I wanted to safeguard their little hearts. But it became clear to me that the path of unforgiveness that I had chosen would end up hurting them in the end. I would like to say that I snapped out of my pain and from that day on I behaved perfectly, but I didn't. I did, however, make a choice that day—a choice to open up every part of me to God for healing and wholeness. The choice was mine; the power to heal and deliver was God's. Jesus met me at the crossroads of love and hate. And as a result of his agape love working in me, I have experienced God doing the impossible in my heart of hearts. I praise God for the narrow road, because it led me into a broad place of freedom.

Did this choice make me uncomfortable? Yes, it did, because it grated against my flesh. Did this choice make everything smooth and wonderful with my ex? No, it did not. Time brought more and more healing for us both, but my choice did not initially seem to speed the process. What did my choice change? It changed me.

Nancy McGuirk speaks of this in her devotional *Rest Assured*: "My natural self would much rather harbor a grudge than forgive. Somehow I enjoy the power of hurting them back, if ever so slightly, by thinking bad thoughts of them or purposely ignoring them. In reality I am only hurting myself because of the consequence of unforgiveness."[3]

I became very aware that choosing *not* to forgive was disobeying God and disallowing his mercy and grace toward me. The choice of forgiveness, though costly, is selfish. When we hold grudges against others, we block our communication with God. Strange as it may seem, forgiving others is the best thing we can do for ourselves. Look at what God's Word says about forgiveness:

> If you forgive men when they sin against you, your heavenly Father will also forgive you. But if you do not forgive men their sins, your Father will not forgive your sins.
>
> Matthew 6:14–15

> Then Peter came to Jesus and asked, "Lord how many times shall I forgive my brother when he sins against me? Up to seven times?" Jesus answered, "I tell you, not seven times, but seventy-seven times."
>
> Matthew 18:21–22

> Bear with each other and forgive whatever grievances you may have against one another. Forgive as the Lord forgave you.
>
> Colossians 3:13

When we choose God's way, he blesses us and honors that choice with more and more of his presence in our lives.

Which Road Will You Choose?

Jesus didn't tell the disciples to follow the crowd, follow their hearts, or follow what seems to be right according to the present circumstance. He simply said, "Follow me" (Matt. 4:19). We only become different when we are following him. We will tend to become more like the one we are following.

A friend of mine began to follow the crowd she was hanging out with. Before too long she felt justified in bad-mouthing her husband and disrespecting him by ignoring his needs. This had its root in a fight they'd had three months earlier. Though the surface was smoothed over, a root of ugliness began cropping up in her heart. Her girlfriends were acting out the same way; why shouldn't she? The sad thing is, these were all Christian sisters, husband-bashing and encouraging each other in their "justified" hurts and ungodly actions. They all were doing it, so they assumed it was acceptable, and it soon became their norm.

We must pay attention to whom we are following. Even though we love our friends and relatives, if they are not committed to following God's commands, their influence can lead us down the wrong path.

As a wild woman, you have a choice. You can just let life happen, which is like serving God your leftovers, or actively run toward Christ and his ways. To run toward Christ is to run away from your own ways. There is nothing casual about this type of living—it is living intentionally. In a tolerant society, this is very wild indeed. This kind of living is passionate, free, unconventional, and courageous!

Jesus said to his disciples, "If anyone would come after me, he must deny himself and take up his cross and follow me.

For whoever wants to save his life will lose it, but whoever loses his life for me will find it."

Matthew 16:24–25

He calls his sheep by name and leads them out. . . . He goes on ahead of them, and his sheep follow him because they know his voice.

John 10:3–4

Follow the way of love.

1 Corinthians 14:1

Because we are all sinners, we all have been guilty of inflicting hurt upon another person. Life happens, and sometimes we get hurt. We need to learn how to live in love despite our hurts. We have some serious choices to make. The first, most crucial choice is this: will I allow this to take me down a bitter road, or will I follow after Christ toward a better road in the middle of this emotional pain?

Emotional pain is hard because no one can see it. We look fine on the outside, but our hearts are twisted up on the inside. When I was in a wheelchair, it was easy for people to see that I was injured. It was obvious. But the women I was speaking to that spring season from my wheelchair carried pain that was not as obvious. They were in their pretty clothes, sitting in beautiful buildings, listening to me speak. But underneath the exteriors were real women with very real hurts in their hearts.

Pain gets our attention and calls out to us, and we must remember that pain always has a purpose. Sometimes it's the pain in the middle of emotional hurt in relationships that propels us to the next wild step with Jesus. When something becomes broken, violated, fractured, or interrupted, we get hurt. This can happen in many ways—people lying, cheating, being unfaithful to us, or allowing their anger to become verbal, emotional, or even physical abuse. In any case, when we are violated, it hurts.

But when we follow Christ in our hurts, we become able to see that the hurt has a purpose. When the hope of purpose amid the pain is evident, we become calmer and much abler to hear the shepherd's voice. He will go ahead of us and show us the way—if we will stop and listen for his voice in the middle of our pain.

Living Up and Learning a Better Way

I can remember a time when my son was hurt by someone in our church. Watching a child hurting brings out the mother bear in us, and it's hard to handle.

This happened at a time in my life when I was learning the importance of walking in God's love and being committed to forgiving others. But this particular instance seemed too much to bear. Within just days I was filled with negative thoughts and ready to lash out if given a chance. And in the course of those days, my focus changed and so did my actions. Instead of living up, I reverted back to devising ways to act out and hurt this person the way they hurt my kid.

It pains me to admit my heart attitude and my desire for ugly actions to vent my anger. During this time God showed me how strong my flesh is within me. I want my way. I even demand it. And if you cross me . . . well, most of you know what happens when someone crosses a woman. But I decided I did not want to be "that kind" of woman. I wanted to live by a higher standard. I needed to go to God's Word and fill my mind with truth like this:

> Make sure no one gets left out of God's generosity. Keep a sharp eye out for weeds of bitter discontent. A thistle or two gone to seed can ruin a whole garden in no time.
>
> Hebrews 12:15 Message

Be careful that none of you fails to respond to the grace of God, for if he does there can spring up in him a bitter spirit which can poison the lives of many others.

Hebrews 12:15 Phillips

See to it that no one misses the grace of God and that no bitter root grows up to cause trouble and defile many.

Hebrews 12:15

We must train ourselves (and it is a discipline) to respond to the grace of God. This is our answer in the middle of our real-life situations. According to Scripture, *not* responding to God's grace is the very thing that allows the bitterness to take root.

How Do I Respond to God's Grace?

When we are hurting it is especially important to get into the habit—yes, habit—of running to the Father with our hurts. He is our safe place. You can tattle up a storm to him about any person. You can tell him how you have been hurt, wronged, lied about, or deceived. You can spell out your mistreatment or the unfair mistreatment you see someone else receiving. And when you go to him with your hurts, you can be certain that he will begin a work in your heart. He will take your bitterness and bring you to a surrendered brokenness. Instead of letting us hold on to grudges and unforgiveness, he will move in us if we will come to him with a heart that is broken over our own sin. Whenever we obey God, he honors it.

Let's see what Paul had to say about being wild:

Love must be sincere. Hate what is evil; cling to what is good. Be devoted to one another in brotherly love. Honor one another above yourselves. . . . Do not repay anyone evil for evil. . . . If it is possible, as far as it depends on you, live at peace with everyone.

Romans 12:9–10, 17–18

As a prisoner for the Lord, then, I urge you to live a life worthy of the calling you have received. Be completely humble and gentle; be patient, bearing with one another in love. Make every effort to keep the unity of the Spirit through the bond of peace.

Ephesians 4:1–3

In humility consider others better than yourselves. Each of you should look not only to your own interests, but also to the interests of others.

Philippians 2:3–4

Our selfishness and shortsightedness will cause us to act in opposition to the flow of God's Spirit. We need to keep ourselves on a short leash, so to speak, when it comes to dealing with others that have hurt us. Do not live in pride. Ask God to empower you to quit thinking life is only about you and what someone did to wrong you. And when it depends on you, live at peace.

Paul shows us that to live wildly as women following Christ we must:

- live a life worthy of our calling
- be humble and gentle
- be patient
- make every effort to keep unity in our relationships
- hate what is evil
- be sincere in devotion
- become a peacemaker

And I think it's safe to say that if we are going to make every effort to keep unity, we will have to set our hearts toward forgiveness.

Choosing Forgiveness

The Greek word for forgive is *aphiemi*, which can be translated "forsake, lay aside, leave, let go, let alone, omit, yield up, put away." These definitions speak something powerful to me.

If I let go of the terrible things that someone does to me, God will also let go of my offenses. Letting go means that I choose to lay the offense aside and give it to God.

If I choose instead to hold on to the things done to me, then I will be guilty of not obeying the will of God. Instead, I will be holding tightly to my own will—my own hurts and my own perceived rights. When I live as one not willing to yield my life situations to my heavenly Father, I am setting myself up for pain and separation from God.

To forgive is also translated as to *yield up*. It is important for us to realize that in our natural selves, we may have a hard time forgiving. Sometimes just a petty thing can send our emotions through the roof. We must always remember that when God asks us to do something and we can clearly see the instruction in his Word, he will give us the grace to carry it out.

Drs. Henry Cloud and John Townsend tell us that forgiveness is a deep process:

> Our well being is intimately tied to our forgiveness of others. It does no good to receive grace with one hand, and deal out judgment with the other. We need to forgive not just with our will but from the heart, from our whole being. Forgiveness is a deeply emotional process whereby we deal with all our feelings. We must be honest about our hurt and anger and not close our hearts and become callous.[4]

Forgiveness is part of the process of our development in Christ. Forgiving is not letting someone off the hook for what they have done; it is trusting God with what they have done. In every situation we have the following options:

- internalize and become bitter
- pay back and try to get even
- forgive and hand things over to Jesus

If you choose—and yes, it is a choice—to internalize your hurts, holding tightly to them, you are allowing those hurts to sour your personality and all that God has created you to be. If you decide—and yes, it is a decision—to pay someone back for the wrong they have caused you, you will be walking in the flesh and not the Spirit. If instead of the first two options you choose—again, it is a choice—to forgive, you will be obeying Christ and walking down that narrow road. You may still remember the situation, but it will no longer have a hold on you.

Forgiveness is the antidote for the poison that begins brewing when we are wronged. Forgiveness is possible when you process the pain of your hurt in the light of God's Word, committing yourself to God.

The moment we start hating others, we become their slaves. When we obsess over the wrongs done to us, we allow the other person to live rent-free in our brains! When we obsess over wrongs done to us, we begin to become more conscious of the wrongs than the good of God in our lives. Doing things God's way will require a lifestyle change.

Once you have chosen forgiveness, you will need to act on your new choice by paying attention to the truth of God's Word, to your actions toward others, and to your mouth and what you say about others.

Your Commitment—Line Up Your Life with Truth

Choosing forgiveness means making a commitment to follow God's way. You may want to stop and pray, asking

God to take the situation you are placing before him and grant you the grace it will take to forgive and lay aside your hurt.

> Forgive us our debts, as we forgive our debtors.
>
> Matthew 6:12 NKJV

Your Actions—Remember That You Will Reap What You Sow

We can all come up with excuses and justifications for our actions. Everyone does it, and for some of us these excuses can be how we justify acting out in the flesh. But if we want to live up and learn a new lifestyle, we will have to pay attention to our actions, because the truth is clear: our actions affect the outcome at every level.

> For with the measure you use, it will be measured to you.
>
> Luke 6:38

Your Mouth—Speak Forgiveness and Bless, Not Curse, Your Enemy

When a physical wound begins to heal, a scab forms, but if it is continually picked off, the wound will never heal. It may even become infected and leave a scar. The same holds true with emotional wounds. Talking about the hurt and the person who caused it is like picking off a scab. It continually reopens the wound and causes it to bleed again. If we want to forgive and recover from hurts and wounds, we must not talk so much about the problem or the person who caused the hurt.

> He who covers and forgives an offense seeks love, but he who repeats or harps on a matter separates even close friends.
>
> Proverbs 17:9 AMP

Men will have to give account on the day of judgment for every careless word spoken.

Matthew 12:36

Bless those who curse you.

Luke 6:28

Let me give you an example of speaking forgiveness. My friend Angie has made a choice to forgive her mother for a lifetime of pain and unimaginable hurt. Her mother is oblivious to the hurt she has caused, but Angie wants to be right with God and pure in her own heart. Before this choice Angie spoke negatively about her mom with her close friends, often making snide remarks, popping off with mean snippets, and joking about the "crazy lady." After making the forgiveness choice and giving her hurts to God, Angie had to stop talking that way about her mom. This was part of her lining up with truth and honoring the choice she made.

If she continued in the negative speech pattern, it would be like picking open the wound, and she would be stuck on an emotional roller coaster. Instead, Angie decided to say nice things about her mom. She looked for opportunities to say something positive instead of living in the familiar negative. This was proof to everyone around her that she was changing. It altered the environment and made way for God to begin healing Angie's heart. Without Angie stirring up bad comments about her mom, there wasn't much to discuss about her with the circle of friends who had heard all the crazy stuff. The negative conversations began to cease, and Angie began to heal and become whole in forgiveness. Though Angie developed appropriate boundaries in her relationship with her mom (because her mom was not a safe person), Angie also had appropriate boundaries around herself—she was not going to settle for unforgiveness or bitterness ever again. Only she had the power to give her mother over to God, and through that daily commitment, Angie's life changed.

Another example of forgiveness being a process and our speech being a clue to where our heart is came in the form of an email that I received from my friend Doug:

> I may have forgiven my ex-spouse three years ago or whenever, but this week something happened to prick me, and I need to forgive her again. Or I may find myself talking about her in a negative light that lets me know that I still have a tinge of unforgiveness left inside. I must go to God again and forgive her. When I hear certain language coming out of my mouth, it tells me that I am hanging on to bitterness. [I pray,] "Lord, I forgive this person, but I need help forgiving them more. Help me to not think so negatively about her. Help me to let go."

Forgiveness is hard because it grates against everything within us. Relationships are often unfair, and yet we are called to choose the higher, wilder road of forgiveness. In the end we win, and in the end it's the best choice possible.

The Balanced Heart

Forgiveness scares us because we think that forgiveness means forging back into a relationship with someone who has wounded us. We must remember that grace is given freely, but trust is earned. We can forgive and release people without giving them unlimited access to our lives. The best example of this I have heard is this: if someone embezzles funds from your company, you can forgive without asking that person to be your future accountant.

As I became convinced that God's way was to let go and forgive, I realized that I had to change my actions. I did this by praying for the person in question every time I thought of them, which was quite often when I was mad or hurt. I kept releasing the person and my hurt to God. I also read and reread verses on forgiveness. And the main thing was to make a wild stand, when necessary, by not engaging in any loose conversation about the person, especially when feeling justified in my pain.

It helped me to have something planned to say, if asked. It was my way of escape from the temptation to go back on my commitment to follow God's way. Forgiveness is life changing because it's walking in the truth—and truth sets a wild woman free. As Beth Moore writes, "With hands freshly loosed, we find liberty to embrace the ONE who never changes, and courage to release those who will."[5]

God has called us to live in his love despite our hurts. Are you wild enough for that?

Wild Strategies for Forgiving and Making Peace

Look Up

- Receive God's forgiveness. People who feel unforgiven are poor forgivers. Begin focusing on God's grace instead of your sins.
- Learn more about forgiveness. Scripture is the best source of information.

Pray Up

- Choose to agree with Scripture that it is God's will that you forgive.
- Ask God to forgive you for holding on to grudges and justified hurts.

Live Up

- Write a letter of forgiveness that you don't send. Get your gut-wrenching dirt out in this private letter. This is for your own healing.
- Relabel those you've forgiven. They are not terrible people. God loves them.

- Get help, if needed, processing intense and painful emotions that accompany forgiveness.
- Thank God for the offender, blessing those who curse you and not repaying any wrong done to you. The blessing is that God is using this relationship or situation to bring you closer to him in an attitude of surrender and obedience.
- As much as it depends on you, live at peace.

Questions for Reflection on the Wild Life

1. Do you have any business to take care of when it comes to forgiving someone?
2. Real Colossians 3:13. What are you told to do, and what are you never to do?
3. Read Matthew 6:14–15. What action is not optional?
4. How many times are you expected to forgive someone (see Matthew 18:21–22)?
5. What is "forgiveness talk," and how do you think you would benefit from it?

7

Wild Women Wear
a Different Style

> You were taught, with regard to your former
> way of life, to put off your old self . . . to be
> made new in the attitude of your minds; and
> to put on the new self.
>
> Ephesians 4:22–24

*M*y friend Beth Ann makes me smile. I love listening to how she processes the things God is showing her. She is certainly a wild woman; she has been surrendering to God in a big way over the last few years, and he has been developing her. As she sits in the developing solution of God's photography studio, the picture of who he created her to be becomes more and more beautiful. As the spiritual seed inside of her grows, her countenance on the outside changes too.

I am a safe person for her to talk to, so from time to time she runs things by me. It has become like trying on clothes so your friend can help you decide what to wear to an event. The difference is that we try on attitudes and responses rather than clothes.

This particular day we were both trying on a variety of styles—love versus bitterness, kindness versus punishing someone, turning the other cheek versus finding a way to take revenge . . . you get the idea. It became our fun little game of trying on attitudes and picking the one God would have us wear as his girls.

Last year Beth Ann gave a great talk at our MOPS group about something she calls "in-fits." She pointed out to the women that most of us know people by what we see on the outside—their outfit. But the most important thing about a woman is her in-fit—what she is wearing on the inside. She spoke of how our in-fit shows. If we are angry, hurt, bitter, resentful, judgmental, negative, discouraged, or depressed on the inside, it will come out—yes, our in-fit shows on us. And if our in-fit is negative or harsh, it doesn't matter how stylish the outfit we are covering up with is. When we are wearing the wrong look on the inside, we are not spiritually in style, and it's not a good look for us as Christians—not flattering or becoming at all.

I was inspired by her talk. It once again made me wonder about my personal choice of in-fits.

Getting a New Wardrobe

As wild women, we're ready for a change of clothing. That's right—a new wardrobe. I bet you never thought that this wild stuff would send you on a shopping spree! That is wild! Well, hold on—I am talking about spiritual outfits, the kind of clothing that lasts the longest and wears throughout eternity.

I am going through my closet and getting rid of clothes that don't fit, are worn out, are dated, or just don't work for me any longer. Some of these items used to be my favorite things. What was I thinking? In fact, I just tried on my longtime favorite blouse. At least it *used* to be my favorite. Today it just hung there and did nothing for me. Though I used to love the color, today I hated it—couldn't even imagine wearing it.

In the same way, we have things in our lives that no longer work for us—habits, attitudes, relationships. Some of these things have hung around in our closets for years, but now they don't fit the new us, the woman who has been "created in Christ Jesus to do good works, which God prepared in advance for us to do" (Eph. 2:10).

To grow in Christ, we learn the basics. Many of us need to *relearn* the basics, because sometimes we never learned or applied them in the beginning. Paul says,

> You were taught, with regard to your former way of life, to put off your old self, which is being corrupted by its deceitful desires; to be made new in the attitude of your minds; and to put on the new self, created to be like God in true righteousness and holiness.
>
> Ephesians 4:22–24

A surefire way to begin acting out instead of living up is to put on my previous in-fit, or my "former way of life," in attitude and action. Paul tells us that our old self is being corrupted by its deceitful desires. The new self is different; it is being created, day by day, to be like God.

Paul uses a familiar action as an illustration. We take things off and put them on every day when we change our clothes. You wouldn't dream of wearing your pajamas to work or out on an errand. You take off your pj's and put on something new for the day. In the same way, let's ask God to change us, making us women who wouldn't dream of going out of the house in our ugly fleshly attitudes. Instead, let's take them off and change them—putting on the new wild woman who is being developed more into his image by the day.

Interior Clothes to Give Away

Most of us need a wardrobe makeover. It's time to give God our hearts and take anything displeasing to him out to the dumpster. Those old clothes, those attitudes not pleasing to God, are not even good enough for charity or a thrift shop— they simply must be thrown out! Francis Chan writes, "By now you've probably realized that you have a distinct choice to make; just let life happen, which is tantamount to serving God your leftovers, or actively run towards Christ."[1] Now let's take a look at a catalog of some possible outfits that can be cleansed or discarded when Christ is our wild new in-fit.

Lying

This in-fit is characterized by untruth or false facts being deliberately repeated to another. It is worn as deceit and falsehood in our character and relationships. The designer of this inward dress is Satan himself, who is known as "the father of lies" (John 8:44). Lying is Satan's style, his native language, and the way he does business. Lying is out of style for the wild woman and certainly not the "right fit" for the woman who is developing spiritually.

You shall not give false testimony against your neighbor.

Exodus 20:16

Keep your tongue from evil and your lips from speaking lies.

Psalm 34:13

You have not lied to men but to God.

Acts 5:4

Therefore each of you must put off falsehood and speak truth-fully to his neighbor.

Ephesians 4:25

Do not lie to each other, since you have taken off your old self with its practices and have put on the new self.

Colossians 3:9–10

In contrast to lying stands truth. Truth is associated with a different designer's style—that of Jesus Christ. Scripture tells us that he is truth, and that truth is the way to be set free from the binding, ill-fitting things in this world (see John 8:32; 14:6).

Anger

This in-fit is characterized by great displeasure, hostility, and wrath. It is worn as yelling and acting out or as passive-aggressive behavior toward the one who is the object of the anger. Though anger is a normal human emotion, what should no longer be normal for the wild woman is the emotion or eruption of anger that spills over to affect her daily relationships and life. A good rule of thumb is a biblical one: deal with your anger at the time, and then move on to the next thing (see Eph. 4:26). When anger spills over into a woman's life, it gives the devil a foothold—a toe into her life.

A fool gives full vent to his anger, but a wise man keeps himself under control.

Proverbs 29:11

An angry man stirs up dissension, and a hot-tempered one commits many sins.

Proverbs 29:22

"In your anger do not sin": Do not let the sun go down while you are still angry, and do not give the devil a foothold.

Ephesians 4:26–27

Everyone should be quick to listen, slow to speak and slow
to become angry, for man's anger does not bring about the
righteous life that God desires.

James 1:19–20

The woman of God looks best dressed in peace and patience. Peace represents our heavenly designer, as he is the
Prince of Peace, and patience is a characteristic of his agape
love—which is the character of God.

Stealing

This in-fit is described as taking something that does not
belong to you. It is worn as unfaithfulness on every level. It's
certainly not becoming for the woman of God.

You shall not commit adultery. You shall not steal.

Exodus 20:14–15

He who has been stealing must steal no longer, but must
work, doing something useful with his own hands, that he
may have something to share with those in need.

Ephesians 4:28

In contrast to stealing is a good work ethic and living hon-
estly and responsibly.

I will never forget Sara, a Christian woman who told me
that God had wanted her to leave her husband and marry
her best friend's husband because they were soul mates. Not
only was Sara stealing another woman's man, but she was
living in deceit. Scripture says we live in the dark when we
don't take off the old and put on the new (see 1 John 1:5–7).
We can justify anything. But the new wild woman in you
will want to make a practice of lining up everything to the
Word of God—truth.

Unwholesome Talk

This in-fit is characterized by speech and conversation that does not build another up. Often worn when we are acting out, this can loosen us up so much that we begin to lose our spiritual focus and grip. Unwholesome speech is never in season for the woman of God.

> Do not let any unwholesome talk come out of your mouths, but only what is helpful for building others up according to their needs, that it may benefit those who listen.
>
> Ephesians 4:29

> Speak to one another with psalms, hymns and spiritual songs.
>
> Ephesians 5:19

The always-stylish wild woman looks for ways to bless others and build them up. But beware, because people—even Christian people—often don't understand this kind of talk or behavior. Again, when the in-fit (speaking a blessing) is biblical, go with that rather than follow the crowd.

Chelsea had one goal every morning: to see how many people she could be a blessing to that day. It didn't matter how they treated her; in fact, the harder the challenge of blessing, the more she pressed in to God for the ability to carry out what only God could do through her. Some days were harder than others, but each day she persisted with her goal of blessing others.

She chose this attitude after being the recipient of some very harsh judgment from other people. She experienced just how defeating it was to be judged and misunderstood. She vowed that she would do whatever it took to learn to live differently—blessing not cursing, giving not getting, and looking at her own shortcomings before dissecting anyone else's life.

Some time ago I wrote down the acts of the flesh (see Galatians 5) on an index card. Seems like a funny thing to commit to memory, doesn't it? But I did this so that I would be very aware of what *not* to line up to and what in-fit *not* to wear as I went through my day. I can still remember a time I was on my cell phone as I drove around doing errands. My friend was complaining about someone, and I was listening and agreeing with her complaint. All of a sudden I remembered that dissension was a work of the flesh. I stopped immediately and told her that the two of us talking about this other person was not fitting for us and not right. What would have been normal before became something that I realized causes great sadness to the Holy Spirit.

Grieving the Holy Spirit

This in-fit is characterized by something that causes deep sadness. A woman grieves (or causes sadness to) the Holy Spirit when she walks, acts, talks, and begins thinking in a way opposed to God. We can clearly see what grieves the Holy Spirit by looking at the works of the flesh.

> The acts of the sinful nature are obvious: sexual immorality, impurity and debauchery; idolatry and witchcraft; hatred, discord, jealousy, fits of rage, selfish ambition, dissensions, factions and envy; drunkenness, orgies, and the like.
>
> Galatians 5:19–21

> Do not grieve the Holy Spirit of God, with whom you were sealed for the day of redemption.
>
> Ephesians 4:30

The contrast to this style of the sinful nature would be to walk in the Spirit:

> So I say, live by the Spirit, and you will not gratify the desires of the sinful nature. For the sinful nature desires what is

contrary to the Spirit. . . . But the fruit of [or the in-fit of] the Spirit is love, joy, peace, patience, kindness, goodness, faithfulness, gentleness and self-control.

Galatians 5:16–17, 22

What we wear on the inside is where the life of the Spirit is. This new clothing puts us in "spiritual fashion" as new women in Christ. If you want to be a fashion statement, this is the best place to start—with your in-fit.

Every Form of Malice

Malice is defined as the desire to harm another. This in-fit can be worn in many ways. It is important that we remember that God's love is not an accessory; it's a foundational garment we must put on each day. It supports us. Love believes the best in everyone; it does not want the worst for anyone. One of the ways to quickly see if you are wearing any malice is to ask yourself if you have become judgmental.

Get rid of all bitterness, rage and anger, brawling and slander, along with every form of malice. Be kind and compassionate to one another, forgiving each other, just as in Christ God forgave you.

Ephesians 4:31–32

It is hard to judge another person if you are kind and compassionate and forgiving toward them. But all of us can be guilty of judgment.

Do not judge, or you too will be judged. For in the same way you judge others, you will be judged, and with the measure you use, it will be measured to you. Why do you look at the speck of sawdust in your brother's eye and pay no attention to the plank in your own eye? . . . You hypocrite, first take the plank out of your own eye.

Matthew 7:1–3, 5

Do not judge, and you will not be judged.

Luke 6:37

Jesus' instruction with regard to judging others is very simply put; He says "Don't."

Oswald Chambers[2]

It's easy to point the finger, isn't it? The trouble is, when we judge others, we pick them apart piece by piece. This not only hurts them but also hurts us by breeding a negativity that grieves the heart of God.

Judging others is something that we all practice much more regularly than we would care to admit. As Oswald Chambers wrote:

> The average Christian is the most piercingly critical individual known. Criticism is one of the ordinary activities of people, but in the spiritual realm nothing is accomplished by it. The effect of criticism is the dividing up of the strengths of the one being criticized. The Holy Spirit is the only one in the proper position to criticize, and He alone is able to show what is wrong without hurting and wounding. It is impossible to enter into fellowship with God when you are in a critical mood. Criticism serves to make you harsh, vindictive, and cruel, and leaves you with the soothing and flattering idea that you are somehow superior to others. Jesus says that as His disciple you should cultivate a temperament that is never critical.[3]

Reclaiming the Right Bags

Remember that luggage I picked up by mistake? I could have worn a man's business suit. I would have been clothed. But it wouldn't have fit, and I would have looked ridiculous. It's just as ridiculous for us to wear our old, ill-fitting habits. Dear wild woman, it won't work for us any longer.

116

Now let me ask you this: Are you ready to clean your interior closet? Do you have some old clothes that are not working for you anymore? Do you have some past lifestyles that need to be tossed?

I think we all probably have some unpacking to do to make room for more of God's rule in us.

- Unpack selfishness—embrace laying down your will.
- Unpack your old self and its attitude—embrace the Spirit life within you.
- Unpack revenge—embrace the truth that God avenges.
- Unpack bitterness—embrace the freedom of letting go.
- Unpack unforgiveness—embrace God's way of grace.

This interior heart-closet reorganization is part of embracing the new kind of wild. Women in Lifelong Development are on the path of change and on the way to freedom! A wild woman has new interior clothes, and she chooses to:

believe truth
hold on to truth
live in the truth
become an extension of truth
live in competence
live in confidence
live in the significance of being God's daughter
live in the security of belonging to him
live as one loved, valued, and cared for

Will you follow me to the dumpster? I have lots of stuff to toss, and Jesus is calling us to follow him, getting rid of every hindrance to the wild life of living up.

Wild Strategies for Wearing a Different Style

Look Up

- What is the in-fit that God would have you wear?
- As you read Scripture, notice heart attitudes throughout.

Pray Up

- Ask for the courage to wear the right spiritual clothing and the determination to make a trip to the dumpster with all the things that are not pleasing to God and are not part of the style he has called you to.

Live Up

- Walk in the Spirit with love, joy, peace, patience, and longsuffering.

Questions for Reflection on the Wild Life

1. Read Ephesians 4:22–24. What are you to put off?
2. What habits or "styles" hang in your closet that need to be dealt with once and for all?
3. Proverbs 29:22 speaks of anger and its outcome. Do you struggle with anger, self-protection, or self-interest?
4. What are you going to unpack?
5. How are you going to put on a new attitude? Create a plan of action.

8

Wild Women Worry Less and Trust More

Live carefree before God; he is most careful with you.

1 Peter 5:7 Message

Stacey once again found herself caught in the middle of real-life stuff. Night after sleepless night, she worried herself to death. She came to see me because she wanted to know how to handle the anxiety that was building up inside of her. She was hoping to blame the problem away or get a quick fix and leave feeling fine. But when I told her that part of our growth in Christ is confronting the habits, thoughts, and activities that do not line up with Scripture, such as our habits of worry, she quickly interrupted with, "Oh, I am just a worrier, have always been—my mother is a worrywart and my grandmother was the queen of worry. I guess I just come by it naturally." As she said with resolve and a smile that it wasn't worry that needed changing but her circumstances that needed an overhaul, I knew we were in for a ride.

I related to Stacey because worry and fear have long been my natural default. I didn't realize that I could live differently, and besides, everyone I knew worried just as much as me. I assumed it was normal. But being a wild woman means confronting the norms of our flesh or our culture that don't line up with God's Word—and so becoming developed in Christ is a long road, with baby-step victories. But every victory counts.

God wants to make a trade with us. He wants us to give him all our cares, problems, and failures—those "ashes" that Scripture refers to (see Isa. 61:3). He then takes our ashes and gives us beauty. He takes our cares, and in exchange, he then cares for us.

> The Spirit of the Lord God is upon me, because the Lord has anointed and qualified me . . . to grant (consolation and joy) to those who mourn in Zion—to give them an ornament (a garland or diadem) of beauty instead of ashes.
>
> Isaiah 61:1, 3 AMP

> Humble yourselves therefore under the mighty hand of God, that he may exalt you in due time: Casting all your care upon him; for he careth for you.
>
> 1 Peter 5:6–7 KJV

God wants to take care of us, but in order to let him, we must stop taking our cares and worries upon ourselves. Often I find myself wanting God to take care of me, all the while worrying or trying to figure out an answer instead of waiting for God's direction. It's like wallowing around in the ashes but still wanting God to give me the beauty. To receive the beauty, I have to give him the ashes of my life.

Worrying is the opposite of faith. It steals our peace, wears us out, and often makes us sick. When we are living in worry, we are not trusting God, and we are not experiencing what it means to enter into God's rest. Hebrews 4:3 says, "For we who have believed (adhered to and trusted in and relied on God) do enter that rest" (AMP). We enter into the Lord's rest through believing.

Privileges I Never Knew

Here's the trade: we give God our problems, cares, and troubles, day by day, and he becomes our place of stability, refuge, and joy. This is the privilege of being his.

It's an offer that most of us don't take advantage of.

For years we have had a credit card that racks up points with every purchase. The points can be used for cash rewards, airline tickets, or gift certificates to some of our favorite places. The card has been in my wallet, but I have only used it occasionally. That was until I found out a friend of mine kept getting free flights, free merchandise, and perks through the same card company. She could not believe that I had the same advantage as she did but never used it. After talking with her about it, I decided to try. It took some organization on my part, like making sure to pay the bill promptly once I used it for my regular monthly purchases, but the reward at the end was worth figuring it out.

In a month my husband and I are flying free to Hawaii, and in a few more months we will be flying free to Palm Springs. In addition, I was able to help supplement a home furnishing purchase with the cash reward I received from the same card company. This has been great! The troubling part is that I had access to these privileges for about five years, and I never used them. Oh, the places I could have gone and the things I could have enjoyed!

That's how it is with us and the Lord. Knowing him and being his daughter has advantages and privileges. But just as I ignored my card, I often let my relationship with him sit idle, not tapping into all that he wants to offer. When he said he came to give abundant life, or life in fullest measure, he meant it. It is on our side that the trouble happens; we simply don't believe him, or we don't want to be bothered with trying to figure out how to claim what is ours.

The Secret Place

God has a secret place and invites us to join him there. This secret place is the place of rest in God, a place of comfort in him. This secret place is a "spiritual place" where worry is erased and peace reigns. It is the place of God's presence. In this place we can dwell in peace and safety. When we spend time in prayer, seeking God and dwelling in his presence, we are in the secret place.

> He who dwells in the secret place of the Most High shall remain stable and fixed under the shadow of the Almighty [Whose power no foe can withstand].
>
> Psalm 91:1 AMP

In the New Testament the Greek word for abide is also translated as "to dwell." When Jesus said, "Abide in Me" (John 15:4 NKJV), he was saying, "Dwell with me." The Amplified Bible translates John 15:7, "If you live in Me [abide vitally united to Me]." In other words, we need to be firmly planted in God. We need to know the Source of our help. We need to have our secret place of peace and security and need to trust God completely.

The secret place is a private place or a hiding place of refuge. We can run there when we are hurting, overwhelmed, or feeling faint. We run there when we are mistreated or are in great need. We can count on our secret place when we just can't take it anymore. God wants to be this hiding place.

Anyone can act out by using other things, such as alcohol or substance abuse, as their hiding place. Some use television, shopping, or eating. Some get depressed and pull the covers over their heads. A lot of people are hiding from the pain of real life. But here's a wild idea: instead of running to other things like the world does, let's learn to run to God. He wants us to find our hiding place in him.

Under His Shadow

According to the psalmist, if we are in the secret place, we will be found abiding "under the shadow of the Almighty" (Ps. 91:1 NKJV). Our heavenly Father doesn't want us to just visit him now and then or run to him only when we are overwhelmed—he wants us to dwell with him, live with him, and remain stable in him. In this place we can remain fixed and focused, because no foe can withstand the power of God.

A shadow provides shade, a place of protection from the sun or heat. The shadow of God acts as the protection from the heat of our real problems. When we work in the hot sun, the shade provides protection, relief, and comfort.

If we decide to stay under the shadow of the Almighty, life is going to be more comfortable. We will still have problems, but in the shade of Jesus, we won't be so miserable, sweaty, thirsty, and dry. Where will you decide to stand?

Stop Worrying

As I was preparing to write this book, I wasn't feeling well. I saw my doctor, who ordered some tests. I got a call not long afterward with the news that my lung X-ray looked suspicious. It showed a spot on my lung the size of a coin and a mass. So I had to go in for a CT scan. They got me in the very same day, but I had to wait through the weekend to find out if that spot appeared to be a malignancy.

123

I have never smoked a cigarette, but my father died of lung cancer and my mother's health was compromised by lung disease. According to my doctor, I had smoked via secondhand exposure for the first eighteen years of my life. The reality of this and the very real memory of my father dying ten weeks after his diagnosis was enough cause for worry. Not to mention that I had a smoker's cough and some breathing issues.

What's a wild woman to do? I decided to use this situation as an opportunity to learn what it would *really* mean to trust God with my life—and to refuse to worry. The next few days changed me.

God had already been teaching me about his provision for even the birds (see Matt. 6:25–34), and I have been using the idea of birds flying unfettered and free in my teaching for the past few years. I even have a little nest in my office to remind me how the birds, safe in their nests, are cared for by God. But this new situation pushed me a step further.

When was the last time you saw a bird sitting in a tree having a nervous breakdown? Have you ever seen a bird pacing back and forth saying to himself, "What happens if God decides to stop making worms today? I will starve to death!" But Jesus told us to look at the birds! They aren't having nervous breakdowns. Every morning they wake up singing and go about their days. They aren't worried about tomorrow; they are too busy taking care of today.

I began once again to watch the birds, and I wondered how much peace people would enjoy if they would take seriously God's promise of provision in every day and in every situation we find ourselves in—whether it's dealing with cancer, financial trouble, marital struggles, troubled teens, broken friendships, addictions, or uncontrollable habits. Wherever we find ourselves today, God tells us not to worry. When we walk around all day saying, "What if, what if, what if?" we are just like unbelievers. Ouch!

Worry Does Not Change Our Situation

Did you ever wonder what your worry accomplishes? Listen to the words of Christ in Matthew 6:27: "And who of you by worrying and being anxious can add one unit of measure (cubit) to his stature or to the span of his life?" (AMP). Oops! Busted!

After I found out I had a spot on my lung, I began to plunge into Internet research on what this coin-sized spot could be. Naturally, the Internet had me dead, or at the very least extremely sick. And naturally, this information was not peace-inducing but a surefire way to stir up the worry. If I continued with the human behavior considered "normal" in a situation like this, I would lose all peace in God. And let me tell you, everyone around me expected me to walk in the "normal" fear and worry, because that is what we do—even as Christians who are claiming to be in God's care.

Why do we worry so much if we believe we are in God's care? Worry causes us to start saying things like "What if?" We begin to fret and begin adding fuel to the fire of our anxious hearts by talking in fear-based rather than faith-based realities.

The first thing I needed to do was to inform my friends that I did not want to receive any negative information—especially from what they found on the Internet—about the lungs. I also did not want to worry, stress, and fret over this. I made it clear that I was going to try something "different." I was going to choose to set my heart and mind on trusting Jesus with my health, the length of my days, and every aspect of the outcome concerning me.

This was hard for some people. Well-meaning friends wanted to find all the research just to inform me how bad this could be. I had to say, "I am so sorry, I can't go there and talk to you about this, but thanks for caring."

I had to take a stand first with myself and then with others, because that is the way people who don't know they have a heavenly Father act. But I know I have a heavenly Father, so I needed to take this opportunity to not only believe it but act like it. And oh, the joy that flooded me when I resolved to keep this upward focus. I was learning to live up in the middle of a real-life storm, and I was growing wilder by the minute.

Each time a fear came to rob my peace, I clung to these verses:

> Therefore do not worry and be anxious.
>
> Matthew 6:31 AMP

> Be anxious for nothing, but in everything by prayer and supplication, with thanksgiving, let your requests be made known to God; and the peace of God, which surpasses all understanding, will guard your hearts and minds through Christ Jesus.
>
> Philippians 4:6–7 NKJV

Prayer is a positive and worry is a negative. When we mix a positive with a negative, we end up at zero.

> But when he asks, he must believe and not doubt, because he who doubts is like a wave of the sea, blown and tossed by the wind. That man should not think he will receive anything from the Lord; he is a double-minded man, unstable in all he does.
>
> James 1:6–8

What a wild thing to see God in everything and to receive everything directly from his hands. Hannah Whital Smith has said,

> We can abandon ourselves to his care; we can trust him fully. Not a sparrow falls to the ground without our Father. The very hairs of our head are all numbered. We are not to be anxious or worried about anything—because our heavenly Father cares for us. We are not to fear, for the Lord is on our

126

side. No one can be against us, because he is for us. We shall not want, for he is our Shepherd. When we pass through the rivers they shall not overflow us, and when we walk through the fire, we shall not be burned, because he will be with us. And it is this very God who is declared to be "our refuge and strength."[1]

Wild Strategies for Worrying Less

Look Up

- "Stop, drop, and roll!" You learned as a kid to do these things during a fire; now apply them to your life. *Stop* every time you are worrying. Physically turn your head up, remembering to look toward heaven for help. Remember him when you are afraid or anxious.

Pray Up

- Next, *drop* to your knees, even if it's just a knee drop in the attitude of your mind. Get before God no matter where you are, and quietly ask him to help you. Pray about each thing on your worry list, as many times as you need to for release.

Live Up

- *Roll* your cares to God and speak truth about what his Word says. You can't live up with your worries when you are always obsessing over them and talking about them. Living up here requires praising instead of complaining.

Questions for Reflection on the Wild Life

1. When was the last time your cast (threw off) your cares to God?

2. What specifically did you have to trust God with? What was the outcome?
3. According to 1 Peter 5:7, what are you to do with your cares and why?
4. Read Matthew 6. What are your conclusions?
5. God is our refuge, our safety from the storms of this life. How can you live this out practically? What should you do when you are anxious or afraid?

9

Wild Women
Stand Firm in Crisis

> God never promised to change our circumstances, but He does promise to change us. He promises to make us victors instead of victims.
>
> Nancy McGuirk[1]

The news came out of the blue: Lorri's husband was facing a job transfer, and within a short time they would be packing up their three children, family pets, and household belongings and moving from northern California to Boulder, Colorado. A lifelong California girl, she initially wasn't thrilled about moving. But over time she not only accepted the change but learned to embrace it as part of God's plan for their family.

Within a few months she was saying good-bye to friends, family, neighbors, her small group at church, and all of us who were near and dear to her. There were laughter, tears, parties, and good-byes, but in the end the Steer family had moved on.

All was well in their new home in the Colorado Rockies until a few months after the move. Lorri found a lump in one of her breasts. A few weeks later, on August 28, she was diagnosed, at age thirty-nine, with breast cancer and scheduled for a double radical mastectomy. During the surgery more cancer was also detected in her lymph nodes and in her other, supposedly clear breast. She was given the diagnosis of stage 3C, which is very serious indeed. Thus began her journey, in a new community, in a new church, with no real friends, through a course of chemo, radiation, and all the things that go with cancer taking over one's life. When Lorri asked what her odds for beating it were, the doctor told her it was a flip of the coin. Not too reassuring.

Despite the circumstances, she continued to remember the day she was diagnosed—August 28—and the picture she had taken that very day of the view from her family room, showcasing the majestic Rockies and highlighting a rainbow that draped the mountains like a colorful curtain. These were the beginning of her "God is with me" story. The date of diagnosis reminded her of Romans 8:28 and the promise she had been learning to hold on to during her move: "All things work together for good to those who love God" (NKJV). The presence of the rainbow reminded her of God's promise to be with his people. This would be the battle of her life, but all things were pointing her to trust in a God who is above and over all.

A few years earlier I had begun wearing a silver bracelet that I had engraved with the simple word "His." I wore this bracelet every day to remind me who I was and whose I was. This reminder began changing me. Women who heard me tell this story often wanted their own bracelet, so I contracted with a jewelry store to make these "His" bracelets, and I take them with me to speaking engagements and have them available on my website. Before Lorri moved away, I gave her a "His" bracelet. It was a special moment and a gift that I knew would come in handy—I had no idea how handy!

She put her silver "His" bracelet on her little wrist and never took it off. This was her daily reminder that she belonged to the Most High God, a heavenly Father who was familiar with human suffering. Every time she saw that silver heart with the word *His*, she would tell herself the truth: "I am his. My life is not an accident; my circumstances are not by chance. I belong to God, and I am loved by God."

Lorri's wild choice to believe she was his in the midst of a terrible life circumstance has inspired many. But it has also unnerved some. Her daily blog, "Terrible and Beautiful: A Daily Web Blog on Cancer, God and Life" (http://lorriscancerup dates.blogspot.com), has inspired many people in the midst of the hardships of cancer, illness, or other disappointments in life. It has also raised some questions. Is she being real? Is she in denial? Is there anyone she is really being authentic with? Is her "pie in the sky" faith something that is genuine or merely a coping mechanism?

Over many months I heard question after question from "strong" Christians who were "concerned" that she was overspiritualizing her situation or in complete denial. I understand their thought process, because there was a time in my life when I thought that people overspiritualized things too much. Now I realize that all of our lives are spiritual—every moment, every circumstance, every choice, every breath.

For in him we live and move and have our being.

Acts 17:28

He doesn't play hide-and-seek with us. He's not remote, he's near. We live and move in him, can't get away from him!

Acts 17:27–28 Message

I believe Lorri is living the wild life. She has not only embraced being in lifelong development, she has embraced cancer as part of what is developing and shaping her. She has faced a crisis with faith, and that is what surprises us. I bet the woman who touched the hem of Jesus's garment looked crazy and a bit desperate, as did Abraham and Sarah, raising children in their old age. They, like us, were normal sojourners who needed direction and hope for living. Like us, they needed faith. Suffering and discouragement brought them to the place of reaching for the Lord's garment—for his presence, for his power.

I am reminded again of the apostle Paul's view on hardship:

> I want to know Christ and the power of his resurrection and the fellowship of sharing in his sufferings, becoming like him.
>
> Philippians 3:10

Was Paul crazy? The word *fellowship* here is from the Greek word *koinonia*, which means partnership, participation, or communion. In the original language *suffering* means something undergone, hardship, pain, emotion, influence, affection, or affliction.

What was Paul saying? Was he looking for crisis? He didn't have to look for trouble; it was all around him. He knew that Jesus predicted it: "In the world you will have tribulation; but be of good cheer, I have overcome the world" (John 16:33 NKJV). And let's face it, Paul was living proof that this life has hardships!

Why would a loving God predict suffering? Wouldn't a loving God want to bless us with good things? This is where our thinking is carnal and not spiritual. We have learned to view life through the lens of the world. We see blessing as good and suffering as evil. Most of us, including me, don't want to go through anything hard. I am sure Lorri didn't pray for cancer, just as I am sure that you haven't specifically asked God for your problems. But life is what it is.

Holding On to the Hope We Profess

In this world we *will* have problems. It's not a question of *if* but a question of *when*. We live in a fallen world, and a very real battle is going on around us—a spiritual battle. As Nancy McGuirk says, "When you hear the words 'red suit, pointed tail, horns and pitchfork,' you think I'm describing the devil, right? Wrong. What I'm describing is the world's caricature of the devil. The danger of seeing that image as a joke, which it is, is that we may also begin to think of Satan's work as a joke, which it isn't. Spiritual warfare is reality, not fantasy."[2]

When Christ died on the cross, a battle was forever won. God defeated Satan. Despite God's victory, the war continues as Satan tries to render believers ineffective through his deceitful ways. He uses the world that we live in because the world's system is opposed to God and caters to the lust of the flesh, the lust of the eyes, and the pride of life (see 1 John 2:16). He also knows how to tempt the flesh, which is our old nature inherited from Adam, a nature that is opposed to God and can do nothing spiritual to please him. There are obvious ways he tries to trip us up—you know the big sins—but those are not the most dangerous. It is far worse to fall into the trap of his subtle appeal in the areas where we are most vulnerable.

Scripture points out that we need to demolish strongholds. What is a stronghold? A stronghold is anything that sets itself up against the knowledge of God. It is anything that exalts itself in our minds and pretends to be bigger than God. Strongholds rob us of our focus and often leave us feeling overpowered. A stronghold consumes much of our emotional and mental energy. Obviously these are the enemy's exact goal—to get us distracted and leave us defeated.

For Lorri, the obvious strongholds would be fear, discouragement, and a longing for the good old days when she was well. If Satan could get her to the place of total defeat, she would give up. But Lorri was determined to walk through this battle with God. Here is an excerpt from her daily blog:

> The real problem of wishing for the good old days is that it robs us of the joy of today. I could completely fall into that trap and starting thinking, "How I wish I was back in Pleasanton, how much better my life was without cancer and moving, and so on and so on and so on." But that would be bitter food for this traveler to glory. That wouldn't be wise. The Bible says, "Don't fret, it only leads to evil." Longing for days gone by is a form of fretting. It's a subtle form of discontentment and that's a very sneaky sin.
>
> Learning to be content, learning to live one day at a time; these are core skills for Christian living. As we learn more and more about how trustworthy and loving and good God is, we will be more and more content with our sustaining manna. When we learn to turn our eyes from the product to the Producer, we'll be much more at rest in the present.[3]

The apostle Paul was a blogger before blogging existed. He wrote:

> We are hard pressed on every side, but not crushed; perplexed, but not in despair; persecuted, but not abandoned; struck down, but not destroyed. We always carry around in our body the death of Jesus, so that the life of Jesus may also be revealed in our body. . . . Therefore we do not lose heart. Though outwardly we are wasting away, yet inwardly we are being renewed day by day. For our light and momentary troubles are achieving for us an eternal glory that far outweighs them all. So we fix our eyes not on what is seen, but on what is unseen. For what is seen is temporary, but what is unseen is eternal.
>
> 2 Corinthians 4:8–10, 16–18

I have watched from a distance as Lorri has embraced her life—illness and all. She is a modern-day example to me of what the older, wiser saints that I read about were probably like. She has not lost heart—two breasts and many months of illness, but never heart. Her heart has remained steadfast.

Where Is the Battlefield?

We see in 2 Corinthians that every crisis presents a real war in our minds. We need to take back any thought that is contrary to truth (see 2 Cor. 10:5). Our mind is the enemy's target because our behavior is influenced by what we spend our time thinking about.

Most women are vulnerable to the things that distract us from turning to God. These are things such as:

- Doubt—questioning God's Word and his goodness
- Discouragement—looking at your problems rather than at God
- Diversion—seeing the wrong things as attractive
- Defeat—feeling like a failure, sometimes so much so that we see no use in trying
- Delay—putting off doing something so that what God has called us to do or what we wanted to accomplish never gets done

These five Ds are tools used by the enemy.[4]

Satan is given names in Scripture. These help identify what he is all about. He is called the tempter (Matt. 4:1–11), the accuser (Rev. 12:7–11), murderer (John 8:44), a roaring lion (1 Peter 5:8), the serpent (Gen. 3:1; Rev. 12:9), the god of this age (2 Cor. 4:4), and one disguised as an angel of light (2 Cor. 11:13–15). And if it were not enough for Satan himself, in all his various ways, to tempt us, the Bible also speaks of Satan's helpers. Paul called them principalities, powers, rulers, spiritual wickedness in high places, and a giant army (Eph. 6:12; Rev. 12:7).

Pay Attention to Truth

One of the most important things to pay attention to on this pathway to spiritual development is the truth. The truth is, we do not battle against human beings. Scripture says we fight against spiritual powers (see Eph. 6:12). We are wasting our time fighting people when we ought to be standing in truth against the devil, who seeks to control people and make them oppose God.

It would be easy to spot the attack or temptation if Satan came to us and said, "Good morning! I am the devil, and I want you to get into something that is going to cause you a lot of misery and will cause you to dishonor your Savior. And if you will only listen to me and obey me, I can accomplish this."

But he doesn't come that way. He seeks to deceive us. To deceive means to cause to accept what is false or to misrepresent the truth. The thesaurus has other words for deceive: double-cross, hoodwink, fool, trick, and dupe. I can't count how many times I have been double-crossed and tricked down a wrong path—and it all starts with one single thought, one single thing left unchecked and unchallenged.

We must remember that there is a very real battle going on, and we must learn to fight the battle God's way, not ours.

> For though we live in the world, we do not wage war as the world does. The weapons we fight with are not the weapons of the world. On the contrary, they have divine power to demolish strongholds. We demolish arguments and every pretension that sets itself up against the knowledge of God, and we take captive every thought to make it obedient to Christ.
>
> 2 Corinthians 10:3–5

We Are Given Grace to Handle Crisis

Here is the most important thing to know: we are different. Isn't that wild? I know, I know, we look into the mirror and we don't look that different—but we are. The Holy Spirit has come to make his residence in us. That is one of the reasons we have become a target for the enemy of God's kingdom. So we must learn to live differently and be aware of the battle we are in. We must also resolve to fight our battles *not* in our own strength but in the strength of the Lord.

In 2 Chronicles 20 we read of a battle aimed at King Jehoshaphat and his armies. Verse 2 says, "Some men came and told Jehoshaphat, 'A vast army is coming against you.'" I don't know about you, but if someone came proclaiming such troubles to me, I would be upset. I am glad to see that I am in good company, because we are told that Jehoshaphat was "alarmed" (v. 3). Alarmed? Yes, alarmed. The people we read about in the Bible were real, flesh-and-blood, scared-of-crisis, wimpy-at-the-thought-of-battle people!

But the story plays out differently than how it would have if I were Jehoshaphat. Yes, he was alarmed, but he tried something that I often forget to do in the middle of a problem—he "resolved to inquire of the LORD" (v. 3). Here is the key ingredient to learning to handle our problems in a new, wild way. What a thought: have a problem, go to God! Don't go to God second, third, or fourth—give him first place and go to him first.

Then Jehoshaphat took it a step further and proclaimed a fast so that all the people could seek help from the Lord. As they all gathered together to seek help from God, he prayed:

> Power and might are in your hand, and no one can withstand you. . . . We have no power to face this vast army that is attacking us. We do not know what to do, but our eyes are upon you.
>
> 2 Chronicles 20:6, 12

This guy was a king, and he humbled himself before the whole crowd of people, admitting that he and his army had no power to fight the battle. Wild? Sure was, because we are conditioned to act big and strong. We carry on like we can handle everything. This mask of being superhuman often keeps us from seeking God. We get so busy trying our own methods that we forget to ask God to intervene. Jehoshaphat not only resolved to seek the Lord but also resolved to stay focused on the Lord. Then God spoke:

Listen, King Jehoshaphat and all who live in Judah and Jerusalem! This is what the LORD says to you: "Do not be afraid or discouraged because of this vast army. For the battle is not yours, but God's."

2 Chronicles 20:15

Listen up, wild women: your battle is not yours but God's. Pay attention and learn a lesson from King J. What are you going through? Are you alarmed, afraid, discouraged? Resolve to seek the Lord and to stay focused on him.

The story doesn't end there. There were more instructions:

You will not have to fight this battle. Take up your positions; stand firm and see the deliverance the LORD will give you. Do not be afraid; do not be discouraged. Go out to face them tomorrow, and the LORD will be with you.

2 Chronicles 20:17

After God spoke to Jehoshaphat, the king bowed to the ground and worshiped the Lord (see v. 18). Wow! The king got scared, humbled himself, sought God, and was blown away when God not only answered but even gave directions. Isn't this a great story? And the story gets played out the same way in our lives too. We seek God and he answers.

Are you ready for the end of this saga? Well, here's a sneak preview—it started with fear and anxiety and ended with praise and peace on every side. Here is what happened:

> Jehoshaphat appointed men to sing to the LORD and to praise him. . . . As they began to sing and praise, the LORD set ambushes against [their enemies]. . . . And the kingdom of Jehoshaphat was at peace, for his God had given him rest on every side.
>
> 2 Chronicles 20:21–22, 30

Imagine this scene. There is a bloody battle coming down, and King J's army is marching behind worshipers who are singing, "Give thanks to the LORD, for his love endures forever" (v. 21). Miraculously, the weaker army, the worshiping army, wins the battle. How? Because God intervened and honored their resolve to seek him, obey him, and trust him. This is very wild indeed.

The next time you are in the middle of a real-life battle and your mind is drowning in the devil's brew, follow God in the heat of the battle:

- Acknowledge God—say, "I don't know what to do, but my eyes are on you."
- Humble yourself before God—admit, "This is too big for me."
- Ask for his help—say, "I need your power and might to battle this."
- Stand in your position as his child—you are known, protected, loved, and valued.
- Be firm—God has empowered you, and God is faithful.
- Do not be afraid or discouraged—these are Satan's tactics to distract you.

- Face the day with faith—God will not leave you; he is present with you.
- Praise him—sing of his love and goodness in the middle of your situation.
- Watch God act—he will set up barriers against the enemy.
- Receive his peace and praise him for his provision.

Living Up Starts with Focus

As I look at this list of things Jehoshaphat did in battle, I see how almost everything has to do with focus. Without the proper focus, we don't see right. Oswald Chambers sums up the importance of our focus:

> The danger comes when, no longer relying on God, you neglect to focus your eyes on Him. Only when God brings you to a sudden stop will you realize that you have been the loser. Whenever there is a spiritual drain in your life, correct it immediately. Realize that something has been coming between you and God, and change or remove it at once.[5]

I can still remember the day I first taught my Bible study class from a wheelchair. I could not do my hair that morning and was feeling too terrible to worry much about makeup. Getting dressed was painful, so I just did the best I could. After being hoisted up onto the stage in a wheelchair lift, I rolled out to everyone's shock. Not many had heard of my injury, so you can imagine how surprised they were to see me in that chair. I wasn't my normal bubbly self. I couldn't move about the stage, couldn't use props, couldn't raise and inflect my voice to grab attention. No, I could not do anything to draw the women in. But God got the attention of all of us. He began speaking to us in such a way that I will never forget that study season. I began to look forward to Wednesdays, to seeing how God would show up.

Shortly after the series was over, I had graduated to a physical therapy called gait training. Yes, it's just as it sounds. I had to learn to walk, or have a proper gait, again. Gait training refers to helping a patient relearn to walk safely and efficiently. Imagine that—I had been walking all my life, and now I had to relearn the very thing that was natural and normal to my daily activity. Gait training is usually done by rehabilitation specialists who evaluate the abnormalities in the person's gait and employ such treatments as strength and balance training to improve the patient's stability and body perception so the patient can walk again without assistance.

Some days it was sweet victory and others sheer frustration. Learning to walk all over again after a lower limb injury was not easy—it was painful. In time I graduated to walking with a cane, and eventually I could walk without any assistance at all. Mission accomplished!

I also graduated spiritually. I was learning how to walk in the wild—in a place and position that I wasn't previously very good at being in. Now when the trials come, I tell myself, "Debbie, take your position and stand!"

What is my position? The same as yours. We are his. We are God's daughters, and as his daughters, we have been empowered to walk in victory in the heat of life's battles. Most people won't understand the peace or the praise, but again, that is what being wild is: daring to walk in truth and light in a world that is filled with darkness.

Lorri wears her "His" bracelet each day with joy for the journey and as a reminder of the God in whom she is held together, cell by cell, breath by breath, day by day. She has not given in to "normal" discouragement but has fought the battle with the truth that she belongs to God and that God can be trusted. As she has said to me, "We are going to go through terrible and beautiful things in life. We can walk through them either with him or without him. I suggest you take his hand."

The apostle Paul reminds us:

Who shall separate us from the love of Christ? Shall trouble or hardship or persecution or famine or nakedness or danger or sword? . . . No, in all these things we are more than conquerors through him who loved us. For I am convinced that neither death nor life, neither angels nor demons, neither the present nor the future, nor any powers, neither height nor depth, nor anything else in all creation, will be able to separate us from the love of God that is in Christ Jesus our Lord.

Romans 8:35, 37–39

Are you ready to take your position, hold on to his hand, put on your God shoes, and stand firm in him?

Wild Strategies for Standing Firm in Crisis

Look Up

- When the battle comes, you will be alarmed—resolve to look up and realize that power and might are in God's hand.

Pray Up

- Do not rely on your own strength. Come into agreement with God's Word that power and might are in his hand. Trust God for your strength and for the outcome.

Live Up

- Wake up each morning and take your position as his girl, and stand firm throughout the day.
- Continue on as if you had victory. You are not a victim—God makes you victorious.
- Refuse to walk in anxiety, worthlessness, incompetence, insignificance, hopelessness, or depression.

Questions for Reflection on the Wild Life

1. What does it mean to stand firm?
2. Read 2 Corinthians 4:8–9, 16–19. Make a note of the condition of life and what our response could look like.
3. Where are your eyes generally fixed?
4. What are the five Ds and how do they play a role in your life?
5. What are we to do when in battle?

10

Wild Women
Confront Fear with Truth

> We must inform our thinking with the Word of God.
>
> Dallas Willard[1]

About a year ago, I was driving down the street when I saw a bumper sticker that read, "Don't Believe Everything You Think." I grabbed a napkin from my purse and quickly scribbled down those words. This simple yet profound little message has changed the way I handle my feelings. I have realized that it's what we think that usually gets us tripped up. My thoughts can take me to places of discouragement, doubt, despair, insecurity, and fear. I know I am not alone.

> Don't become like the people of this world. Instead, change the way you think.
>
> Romans 12:2 GOD'S WORD

Jennifer was sure she was going to be fired from her job. Though nothing in particular added up to that estimation, she was certain her boss was unhappy with her and her co-workers only tolerated her. This nagging fear of pending rejection caused her a lot of secret stress. She tried harder than ever before with every assignment she was given, but still that nagging sense of not being supported, appreciated, or even wanted by her employer persisted.

She thought long and hard about the situation, and her emotional state moved from hurt to mad to completely bitter. Then one day, out of the blue, something someone said seemed to pull the trigger on her pent-up emotional tank. She let loose, said things she still can't believe she said, acted out in ways she is still embarrassed of, and quit with no notice—shocking everyone she worked with.

Her co-workers were left with lots of questions. They loved her and thought she did an amazing job. It seemed impossible that she could have snapped like this and even more impossible that she would quit a job she had repeatedly said she loved. What happened?

Jennifer didn't surface again for many months. She knew that her own actions had ended up hurting her more than any person ever could. Her actions were a direct result of how she mentally spun her situation with a negative thread. And though at the time that negativity appeared to be directly caused by her work environment, the truth was, her negativity was a habit of a thought process that she had never been aware of or addressed. The negative spin she found herself in was really about her personal insecurities and her need to feel important and validated. Her job left her feeling slighted, not included, and not as valued as she yearned to be. Instead of trusting these feelings to God and learning to sort them out on a personal level, she projected and made a mess of things—a mess that ended up drawing her into a season of depression.

Months later she told me that she had believed, really believed, that no one wanted her there anymore and that she was driving everyone crazy. When faced with her perceived pending rejection, she "acted out" and snapped. She just couldn't figure out why she felt that way, so she assumed it was the truth.

Are you always trying to figure everything out? Many of us fall into that trap. Instead of giving our cares to the Lord, we go through life carrying our cares, obsessing over our cares, and allowing our cares to take us places that we don't need to go. When we are trying to figure everything out for ourselves, we are exalting our reasoning above God's wisdom. We are acting and living like we are the smart ones and God is just there to mop up any messes we might make along the way.

What would it be like to live as if God is the smart one?

> Trust in the LORD with all your heart
>   and lean not on your own understanding;
> in all your ways acknowledge him,
>   and he will make your paths straight.
> Do not be wise in your own eyes,
>   fear the LORD and shun evil.
> This will bring health to your body
>   and nourishment to your bones.
>
> Proverbs 3:5–8

Over the past couple of years I have realized how much I gravitate to leaning on my own understanding for most everything. I take great stock in my thought processes and ideas. I know that this is normal and that everyone does this. But the Lord began speaking to my heart and planting a wild thought in me: *What if leaning on your own understanding is the very thing that keeps tripping you up with discouragement, distraction, and fear? What if your own understanding is still skewed from past hurt, dysfunction, and emotional baggage? What if your own understanding is unspiritual?*

What exactly does it mean to lean on our own understanding?

lean: to rely on for help or support, to rest
your weight upon

understanding: perception, comprehension,
thinking capacity, or feeling

What is thinking? "Thinking is a powerful gift of God to
be used in the service of truth."[2] It is the activity of searching
out what is true in light of given facts or assumptions. We
must learn the importance of informing our thinking with
the Word of God. We must learn to take the Word in, dwell
on the truth of God's Word, and ponder its meaning and
its implications. Then we need to explore its application to
our very own everyday life. In other words, we must make it
a goal to put God's Word in our brains to think about, then
put it into practice. This is how we focus our mind on God
and his ways.

Our Thinking Educates Our Feelings

Change begins in our thoughts. Our thoughts hold ideas, images, and stored-up information—all important for women
in the process of spiritual development to look at. Because
we are free and not robots, we get to choose what we let our
minds dwell on. We have the responsibility to try to keep
God in the front of our minds—even if we do this in a stop-
and-start fashion. If we begin to habitually put Christ in our
thoughts, we will make progress toward developing spiritually
and moving toward him.

A battle is going on in our mind (see Eph. 6:12). These
powers work in the idea systems, like our thinking—the part
of us that makes assumptions about reality. This idea system
makes up our pattern of thinking, and our thoughts lead
to our feelings, which in turn take us to the realm of our
actions—or our acting out.

We are not supposed to rely on our own feelings, putting too much weight on them, because they have been impacted by a human mind that is often led by the flesh and not the Spirit. When we are leaning on our own understanding, we are *believing everything we think*. And the life instruction I see in Proverbs 3:5–8 is that we are *not* to believe or buy into everything we think. We are not to lean on our own understanding (perception, comprehension, feelings, or thoughts). Basically, we are being told that we are not to try to figure things out based on what we feel or see. What Proverbs is saying is that we are to learn to live by faith.

> Faith comes from hearing the message, and the message that is heard is what Christ spoke.
>
> Romans 10:17 GOD'S WORD

> The righteous will live by faith.
>
> Galatians 3:11

I like Eugene Peterson's translation of this in *The Message*: "The person who believes God, is set right by God—and that's the real life" (Gal. 3:11 Message). If we are going to live in a spiritual reality that impacts our reality here on earth— the way it was set up to—we will have to begin believing God. We cannot believe God until we know *what* to believe. The good news is, it's not a secret. It is clear and at our fingertips; we just must become convinced that the way to real life is through faith and that faith comes from hearing God's Word. When we fill our minds with God's Word, our feelings begin to change too.

Many of our feelings, emotions, and desires must be changed if we are serious about spiritual development. Stay with me—I know this is hard to grasp because we live in a world that is all about our feelings. Not relying on myself and what I feel doesn't seem very practical and certainly seems a little weird. Now here comes one of those wild exchange moments again: instead of trusting myself, my thoughts, and my emotions, I am to trust in the Lord with all of my heart and acknowledge him in all of my ways (see Prov. 3:5). I am to plant truth where there once was none: in my mind.

Most of us know that this verse is in the Bible, but how many of us have picked it apart and tried to understand and live by what it is saying to us? If we did, it would make a wild difference. The promise that follows the command is that if we trust God instead of ourselves and acknowledge him in everything, our paths will straighten out.

Here's Eugene Peterson's paraphrase of these verses:

> Trust God from the bottom of your heart;
>   don't try to figure everything out on your own.
> Listen for God's voice in everything you do, every-
>   where you go;
>   he's the one who will keep you on track.
> Don't assume that you know it all.
>   Run to God! Run from evil!
> Your body will glow with health,
>   your very bones will vibrate with life!
>
> Proverbs 3:5–8 Message

This change does not happen overnight or with the snap of a finger. Making a decision to follow Christ with our thoughts and commit our feelings to him is radical—and yes, very wild. Many women cannot imagine who they would be without the fears, anger, lusts, power plays, bitterness, depressed moods, and inner wounds that have kept them locked up in self for so long. Part of their identity is tied up in these habits of thought and feelings.

I know what this is like because I carried around feelings of rejection for so many years, believing that being the "not enough" girl was part of my identity. It has taken years of putting truth in the place of lies to change what I believe about myself. I had to turn what I thought around to what was true according to God. I am not speaking of a renewed self-esteem. I am speaking of a changed belief system that is rooted and grounded in Christ and his love. Dallas Willard addresses this:

> Our initial move toward Christ-likeness cannot be toward self-esteem. Realistically, I'm not okay, and you're not okay. We're all in serious trouble. That must be our starting point. Self-esteem in our situation will only breed self-deception and frustration. Regardless of what we may say to "pump ourselves up" or what others might tell us, we are better off not concealing or denying who we really are.[3]

Who I really am is a woman who in herself gravitates toward the sin nature that leads her down a path of self-seeking and eventual emptiness. Who Christ really is—through his death and resurrection—is the answer to my sin nature, desiring to lead me down a path of seeking righteousness and eventual fullness.

Christ doesn't come into our lives and ask us to quit feeling. Feelings are part of being human. Feelings move us and give us a sense of being alive. In the absence of feelings, we would not have any interest in anything. Feelings are an essential part of life. So as women in lifelong spiritual development, we are to take good care of our feelings and not just let them "happen."

Destructive Feelings Are Alive and Well

Many of the feelings that we have learned to live in are not healthy for us or others. We need to lay down our thoughts. Second Corinthians 10:5 tells us that we are to "take every thought away captive into obedience of Christ." We are to cast our cares on him and avoid human reasoning (Prov. 3:5–7). When we do that, we will stop trying to figure everything out and will learn to enter into his rest. "For we who have believed (adhered to and trusted in and relied on God) do enter that rest" (Heb. 4:3 AMP).

If we are not resting, then we are not believing and trusting, because the fruit of belief and trust is rest. Whenever I am trying to figure everything out, I know I have stopped trusting God in a matter. This is easy to do with my four adult children whom I love deeply. They are all at different places in their lives, and I could make myself crazy over their decisions, their futures, and the areas in which they need some growth. Each time I start this thinking cycle, I stop. I ask God to forgive me, I admit that he is God and I am not, and then I give my care for my children completely over to God. I imagine myself leaving it there with him and walking away. I can only do this when I remember that he is faithful and will work in each situation of my life.

I have realized that I have to give up my habit of excessive reasoning. God has told me recently to make some changes in my life. He has confirmed it in many ways several times. I have no idea what those changes look like. It has been driving me crazy that I don't know where God is taking me or what changes he will ask me to make. Some days I have worked myself up into a tummy knot! I would assume this means that I have not given my reasoning over to his hands. I still plot and plan and analyze my steps. He keeps saying, "Follow me," but somehow those words don't seem enough. So I turn the other way and keep overthinking. Again he says, "Follow me. Debbie, pay attention to me." I am finally getting it and am thrilled with the freedom and absence of worry or foul moods!

The book of James points out how feelings lead to drama in the lives of believers:

> What causes fights and quarrels among you? Don't they come from your desires that battle within you? You want something but don't get it. You kill and covet, but you cannot have what you want. You quarrel and fight.
>
> James 4:1–2

The causes of such conflicts are the underlying feelings involved, which will only surface again if denied or stuffed down. Proverbs has wisdom about the good and bad produced by the feelings in our lives. Take a look.

> When pride comes, then comes dishonor (see Prov. 11:2).
>
> Anxiety in a man's heart weighs it down (see Prov. 12:25).
>
> Hatred stirs up strife, but love covers all trangressions (see Prov. 10:12).
>
> A cheerful heart has a continual feast (see Prov. 15:15).
>
> A joyful heart is good medicine, but a broken spirit dries up the bones (see Prov. 17:22 NASB).
>
> The fear of man brings a snare (see Prov. 29:25 NASB).

Negative feelings originate from negative thoughts that have gone unchallenged. When left unchecked, the negative takes over, and we begin to believe what we think. Before long the feelings take root and spread into other areas of our life. They spread like yeast and may even determine the immediate outcome of things in our lives or our relationships with others.

Our moods are affected by what we think. What we call moods are feelings that take over. Anger, fear, insecurity, doubt, and bitterness start as thoughts that become feelings and can become a permeating mood. On the positive side, feelings and moods that are associated with truth can spread and permeate us too. When we believe we "belong" and have purpose, we begin to experience what it means to feel that we really are accepted. To say we are the beloved of God is simply to state that we are dearly loved by him. The foundation of our faith rests on this love of the Father toward us. When we believe that we are the beloved, dearly loved women that Scripture says we are, we change. Confidence, worthiness, love, hope, joy, and peace can all spread wildly within us, making a difference in the way we think, in the way we feel, and ultimately in the way we act and relate.

Jesus Makes Us Different

Remember the fishermen? Jesus kept calling them to something different: *follow, believe, give me your nets, step out in the water, sit with me, pray with me, be with me.* He called them to become different people because they were in an apprenticeship with the Son of God. We are being asked to be in an apprenticeship too. We are like interns, learning how to live in Christ. Our teacher is the Master himself. We cannot touch him or see him like those first disciples could, but we have his Spirit living within us—leading and guiding us into all truth.

Jesus asks us to trust him with our cares, and he, in turn, will make our paths straight—will make a level path for us to walk on. Any way we look at it, when we follow Jesus—in steps, vocation, thoughts, decisions, or calling—he makes us something different.

God has never called me to figure out my life; he has just asked me to come to him and follow him. When real-life problems or situations happen, I am to:

- trust him with all my heart;
- turn from my own understanding, feelings, and reasoning;
- instead, acknowledge him in the situation;
- and he will make the way straight.

What about you? What have you been thinking about lately? How are your moods and attitudes? Can you follow him into the unknown, just because he says he is God?

It's wild, isn't it?

153

Wild Strategies for Not Believing Everything You Think

Look Up

- Remember that not every thought that comes to you is good for you.
- Examine your thoughts next to the truth found in Scripture.
- Notice that the negatives do not line up with truth.

Pray Up

- Ask God to help you divide the good from the bad, casting all thoughts and processes before him.

Live Up

- For every stray thought that is not captured, a stray emotion will pop up. Learn to be discerning with your own thoughts.
- Recognize the thoughts that are trapping you and are not productive.

Questions for Reflection on the Wild Life

1. What does Romans 12:1–2 say we are to do?
2. How do your thoughts affect your actions?
3. What thinking can easily get you off track?
4. Part of living up is the transformation that Romans 12 speaks of. Read the entire chapter and note the key points regarding a transformed life.
5. How do you bring a thought under the obedience of Christ?

Part
Three

Determined

*Finding Courage to Follow
a New Path*

The path of life leads upward for the wise.

Proverbs 15:24

Living up requires following a new way.
Living up is about putting our self aside.
Living up is contrary to acting out.
Living up is life in the Spirit—acting out is life
in the flesh.

11

Wild Women
Have a New Groove

The giant step in the walk of faith is the one
we take when we decide God no longer is a
part of our lives. He is our life.

Beth Moore[1]

*J*ust when I thought it was safe to walk normally, life
happened—again! For almost a year I couldn't walk
around normally. I either had crutches, a cane, or an orthopedic boot. Once I finished my gait training and fully recovered,
I couldn't have been happier. But my full recovery was short
lived. Just a month after my right leg seemed normal, about
eleven months after the original injury, I could not step down
on my left foot. I couldn't believe it.

I wound up with what seemed like a sympathy injury, and
a very painful one at that. This time the tendon that wrapped
around the ankle of the other leg tore, requiring surgery,

a cast, and bed rest for six weeks. I needed a wheelchair, crutches, and so on for a second time. This second injury was worse than the first. All I could think was, *You've gotta be kidding me. I can't believe this is happening*!

I faced my second consecutive spring in a wheelchair. Due to the nature of the injury, I had to learn to walk all over again—again. This second time around I discovered even more parallels between physical gait training and learning to walk spiritually.

I'd been a Christian for many years, but now my life came apart at the seams. I talk about that part of my life in the book Deeper, but to sum it all up, let's just say that in 1990, after seventeen years of being a Christian and serving in ministry for most of those, I needed to learn to walk with Christ all over again, and I am still learning. I guess you can say that I had to learn a new rhythm and a new groove. Eugene Peterson says,

> Not only do we let God be God as he really is, but we start doing the things for which he made us. We take a certain route; we follow certain directions; we do specified things. There are ethical standards to follow, there are moral values to foster, there are spiritual disciplines to practice, there is social justice to pursue, there are personal relationships to develop. We will not do any of this perfectly and without fault. But that isn't the point. The way is plain—walk in it.[2]

Webster's defines a groove as a long, narrow channel. I think that obedience is much like that long, narrow channel or groove. Certainly God is calling us to a narrow road. Or as I like to think of it, he is calling me to the dance floor, but my only partner is to be him. It's a single-focused relationship with an undivided heart and a new way to live. And if I am going to dance, I will need to get a new groove on!

This kind of fidelity is narrow. It's wild to think that we can be faithful to a God we cannot see. There is no provision for dating or flirting with another partner. Jesus wants to be mine and wants me to be his—and he wants to lead you to the dance floor too. God himself has called our name, extended his hand, and invited us to dance with him and partner in the work he is doing in the world.

If I am going to dance, I think I need dance lessons! But in this dance with the Father, it's not as much about dancing as it is about loving him. As Ken Gire says, "The Christian life is about intimacy, not technique."[3] The Lord of the Dance wants us to go with the music, fall into his arms, and follow his lead. This dance invites us to a more intimate relationship with him.

Dancing to a New Rhythm

All of us have life rhythms that define our days, our habits, and our personal style of living. For several years now, I have had a busy and sometimes intense schedule. I had thought that I'd figured out how to make it all work—family in check, house in order, marriage flames kept burning, and time with God. But God was calling me to more. I had been dancing with him on a crowded dance floor with a party of other people. Now he wanted to take me into the candlelight and dance with me slowly and intimately and have me all to himself. I suppose that might have been what he wanted when the first injury happened, but I will never know. All I know is that when it happened the second year in a row, he got my attention.

Lord, did I miss something the first time around? Did you want something from me back then? Are you trying to get my attention? I am listening. You have me. You have all of me, with a leg cast and on complete bed rest. What are you asking of me, Lord?

Then a wild answer came very quickly: *No visitors.*

What? Did you say I am not to have visitors?

No visitors.

Whoa! That certainly sounded like a real bummer. I kept questioning like a pestering child: *I am to be in complete bed rest this time around with no visitors? No keeping speaking engagements, no friends keeping me company, no visitors?*

God's direction was very, very clear. So I told my friends that I was not taking visitors but would appreciate their prayers while I was in bed. They brought meals but never came upstairs to my room. At times it drove me crazy. I am a people person, and I wanted to jump up and visit. But God said no visits. One thing I know—they must have prayed!

I cannot put into words what happened when God got me alone and to himself for that extended period of time. I had no responsibilities, no visitors, and no schedule to keep, and I could not even walk around and get distracted. He had me on the dance floor, and he was giving me private lessons. If I missed it this time (and I could have), I not only would have missed the dance, I would have missed the romance.

Frederick Buechner once wrote that the gospel is part tragedy, part comedy, and part fairy tale. The tragedy is that we have estranged ourselves from God, making us unlovable. The comedy is that even so, he has invited us to the ball. The fairy tale is that not only are we invited to the ball, but we will be transformed so that we will be fit for the ball.

With me alone in my room, day after day, God was doing a work of transformation, making me fit for the ball. He was showing me how to take care of myself spiritually, what to wear in attitude, and what action steps to take in the dance. All of these things were, in a spiritual sense, a wildly delicious mix of spirit and adventure—a mix of love, hope, and joy; a combination of real life and real faith.

In the little book *My Heart—Christ's Home*, Robert Boyd Munger compares our hearts to a place where Christ comes and makes his home. As a person gets busier, they spend more time rushing about and not much time sitting by the fireplace with Jesus. He portrays Jesus saying:

> The trouble is that you have been thinking of the quiet time, of Bible study and prayers, as a means for your own spiritual growth. This is true, but you have forgotten that this time means something to me also. Remember, I love you. At a great cost I have redeemed you. I value your fellowship. Just to have you look up into my face warms my heart. Don't neglect this hour if only for my sake. Whether or not you want to be with me, remember I want to be with you. I really love you![4]

As I read this I realized that once again, in my life, my time with Jesus had been reduced to something I checked off a list of duties rather than a journey stemming from desire. Betty Skinner had journeyed this path before me, with a different injury but the same calling to solitude and transformation. She says:

> Trust and letting go work mysteriously together. Nothing ever stays the same in our lives, and again and again we are called to let go in order to find a new way. If we continue to cling to the past and never dare to let go, we will never learn to trust. If we never trust, we will never dare to let go. Our choice is this: to become more bound up trying to fight the reality we find ourselves in and hold on to our illusion of control, or to become more free by trusting God's goodness and desire to move us to a new place of freedom. . . . We have to let go of how we perceive that things and people in our life should be, take off our god-coats and let God be God.[5]

She goes on to say that the first step is submission—surrender to God—and the second is to allow some time for God to work and circumstances to unfold. I have found this to be the new groove of walking in and waiting on the Spirit in my personal life.

Call to the Wild—Women in Lifelong Development

Peter lays out a spiritual development plan in 2 Peter 1:3–11:

> His divine power has given us everything we need for life and godliness through our knowledge of him who called us by his own glory and goodness. Through these he has given us his very great and precious promises, so that through them you may participate in the divine nature and escape the corruption in the world caused by evil desires.
>
> For this very reason, make every effort to add to your faith goodness; and to goodness, knowledge; and to knowledge, self-control; and to self-control, perseverance; and to perseverance, godliness; and to godliness, brotherly kindness; and to brotherly kindness, love. For if you possess these qualities in increasing measure, they will keep you from being ineffective and unproductive in your knowledge of our Lord Jesus Christ. But if anyone does not have them, he is nearsighted and blind, and has forgotten that he has been cleansed from his past sins.
>
> Therefore my brothers, be all the more eager to make your calling and election sure. For if you do these things, you will never fall, and you will receive a rich welcome into the eternal kingdom.

Being wild starts with God's divine power, which has provided everything we need for life and godliness. Then it proceeds to the precious promises that make it possible for us to partake in the divine nature. Then there seems to be a pattern, or new groove, laid forth for us:

1. Put forth your very best effort ("make every effort," v. 5).
2. Add faith, goodness, and knowledge (see vv. 5–6).
3. Live in truth by practicing self-control (add to knowledge, self-control; see v. 6).
4. Live in self-control by adding perseverance (patience under pressure; see v. 6).

5. Persevere in the wild life by adding godliness (participate in the divine nature; see v. 7).
6. Grow really wild by living in kindness and gentleness (brotherly love; see v. 7).
7. Be fully developed in agape love (God's unconditional love; see v. 7).

Peter concludes by saying that if we do these things we will never stumble and will be welcomed into the eternal kingdom (see vv. 10–11).

Spiritual development requires both God's effort and ours. He tells us to do some things, and at other times he tells us to choose. We apply diligence to training ourselves to do what is good and right. This is something we must do; it will not be done for us. We must add knowledge—again, this is something we must be part of. The Bible doesn't fall from the shelf each morning and open for us. We must put the Word of God into our minds, and then God's Word, which is alive, will do the amazing work of developing and transforming our minds.

God has a provision system. He has given us divine resources and has put his Spirit within us. We work from a place of victory, power, and strength—all his provisions. Our part is to follow as he guides. His part is to make the wonder-working, sanctifying difference in our lives.

God's Planning System

I have a terrific neighbor and friend named Terry. She often helps me with ministry-related things and travels with me to speaking engagements. When we go by car, she often offers to drive. This past Christmas her husband gave her a fancy new car with all the bells and whistles—including a high-tech navigation system.

My car is ten years old and doesn't talk to me. The only navigation system I have is me, and I am directionally challenged. Trying to find my way is often a riot.

I had my first experience with a GPS on a recent trip with Terry. We had been to this retreat center before and knew where we were going, but she wanted to play with her new toy, so she entered the destination address into the GPS. As we were driving down the freeway, the little lady in the box began to speak up: "In a quarter of a mile, exit to the right."

We didn't believe her. We knew where we were going, so we ignored the lady and did our own thing. The trusty navigation lady recalculated our route since we didn't obey her directions. So we drove on, happy that she saw things our way, until she spoke again: "In one mile, exit the freeway to the right."

We couldn't believe it. She got it wrong again. We both shouted, "No way!" and we sped ahead like rebellious teens. The little lady patiently rerouted our trip, seeing it our way.

Whew! She had finally gotten in sync with us. Before too long, she told us to get off right where we thought we should. We arrived at the retreat center, smug in the knowledge that we beat the little lady in the GPS. But we found out later that the first two exits were both quicker routes that we didn't know about. Insisting on following our own way took us a little longer.

I have to admit that the little lady in the box was driving me crazy after a while. I just wanted her to shut up. If it were my car, I would have to give her a name, because I know if she talked to me all the time, I would be talking back! I later found out that technology does have its blessings. The navigation system can be turned off. One push of a button and the little lady leaves you alone to fend for yourself behind the wheel!

This is a lot like our lives. We think we know how to get where we are going. We devise a route, a course, a map. God intervenes and gives us some different instruction, but we say, "No, Lord—thanks, but I know what I am doing and where I am going."

In his love he keeps recalculating our course. He wants to get us back on track. But he never takes away our ability to choose. Nevertheless, he is patient when we keep going our own way.

Sometimes we opt to turn off his guidance. We tell the Lord, "I just don't want to hear you anymore!" But just like the navigation system, God's GPS is ready and waiting for us to choose to hear his voice again.

We have been trained to do things our own way. Old habits die hard. So we live life doing the best we can. God has a navigation system too. It's a GPS, all right—God's Planning System and God's Provision System.

In his planning system he says, "I will complete that which concerns you" (see Ps. 138:8 AMP). And tenderly speaking to us in Isaiah 46, he says:

> You whom I have upheld since you were conceived,
>   and have carried since your birth.
> Even to your old age and gray hairs
>   I am he, I am he who will sustain you.
>   I have made you and I will carry you. . . .
>   I say: My purpose will stand.
>
> vv. 3–4, 10

In his provision system he says, "I have given you everything you need for life and godliness" (see 2 Peter 1:3); "I will never leave you nor forsake you" (Josh. 1:5); "I will supply all your needs according to my riches" (see Phil. 4:19).

It's all about following—following his lead.

Wild Strategies for Living in a New Groove

Look Up

- Recognize that God has all the divine power and re-sources you need for every area of your life.

165

Pray Up

- Ask him to be your provision, your guidance, your everything.
- Ask him to lead you and guide you each day.
- Ask God to teach you how to dance the dance of faith.

Live Up

- Obey his voice.
- Follow his lead.
- Act quickly when he nudges you.
- Put on those faith dancing shoes!

Questions for Reflection on the Wild Life

1. Read 2 Peter 1:3–11. What does this passage say to you about living in a new groove?
2. When are you most tempted to "suspend guidance"?
3. What would it be like to really believe and trust that God has the best route mapped out for us?
4. What would it be like to be daring enough to step out onto the dance floor with only him?
5. What part of you is God requiring surrender of today?

12

Wild Women Capture the Sparkle in Life

A daily recommitment is not to ensure that we'll never fail, but to help us develop the mentality that every single day is a new day. A new chance to follow Christ.

Beth Moore[1]

*R*emember the memorial service I didn't get to attend? Well, to make up for that, let me tell you a little bit about my friend Sherrie and what I would have said to the crowd of family and friends if I hadn't made an unplanned trip to the emergency room that day.

Sherrie had served on our women's ministry core team for several years. She led Creative Hearts, which was the women's crafts ministry. We are not talking just any ol' crafts here; we are talking beautiful mosaics, creative quilts, and other

167

memorable pieces that women enjoyed getting to learn how to make.

But Sherrie didn't just know crafts; she also knew a lot about cancer. She had been diagnosed with melanoma and had it successfully removed many years before. But the melanoma came back, as it sometimes does. The doctors told Sherrie she had only a short time to live. It was November, right before the holidays, and Sherrie was understandably devastated.

She went through the holidays with gloom and doom in her mind. Her attitude was dark, she became increasingly depressed, and in her words, she was hard to be around. She didn't want Christmas, for goodness' sake—she was dying! But she didn't die. She lived on an "everything is off-limits" diet and holistically fought the cancer within her. She was no longer a statistic.

A few years later, at the exact same time of year, Sherrie's cancer returned, this time revealing itself in the form of a seizure. The melanoma had spread to her brain. That November Sherrie was told she had weeks to live. But something was different this time around. Sherrie got wild about her life and made a radical decision. Sherrie decided that she wasn't going to waste her final weeks having another black Christmas. This time she vowed to herself and to God that she would not miss the sparkle of each day.

She would see it in every twinkling Christmas tree, in every beautiful bow and package, in every smile, every person, and every event. She was determined to go out seizing the sparkle—every last ounce of sparkle—in her life.

We were all amazed at her courage to face death with such resolve and inspired by her joy—pure joy—as she sought to live out her last days being happy in the God she loved and spent her life serving.

Admittedly, Sherrie hadn't always lived in the sparkle of life. Like most of us, she could get discouraged and negative. But now she was showing us how to live through her death.

She began to affectionately call her prognosis her "shelf life" and her death her "expiration date"—even laughing that both were coming soon.

I have a favorite story about Sherrie's last days. On one Sunday morning her husband, Don, brought her into church in a wheelchair. The melanoma had spread into her nervous system and affected her ability to walk. She had on a sparkly Christmas sweater, and her wheelchair sported a Christmas wreath. When she saw our women's staff across the courtyard of the church, she yelled out to Beth Ann, "Beth . . . I have hospice now!"

We looked at each other in disbelief. She was excited to have hospice? When we realized this was the truth, we just looked at each other and said out loud, "She is excited to have hospice!"

Earlier in the month Sherrie had asked Beth and I if she could give us a private concert. A soloist in her earlier days, Sherrie spent many of her later adult years discouraged that she did not have an outlet for her gift of song. But when she decided she wasn't going to miss the sparkle, all that changed. She decided to do a private concert for us, complete with a pianist, in the small chapel of our church. As she stood by the piano, singing victoriously and with joy, Beth Ann and I both had tear-stained faces. We knew what this performance meant to her. She wasn't missing the sparkle—in anything!

We have all picked up her famous little tag line: "Don't miss the sparkle." We remind each other of the truth, we wear sparkly accessories, and we often think of Sherrie's impact on us during those last weeks.

Right after her memorial service, I put a very large and very sparkly brooch on the boot that I had to wear on my right leg. I placed it prominently at the strap on top, where it would remind me many times during the day that I was to rejoice—even in the pain. The next year, I put that sparkle pin right back on my left cast and then my boot. I needed the reminder. Rejoicing—not missing the sparkle—was something new for me. Rejoicing meant not caving in to my feelings, emotions, or thought processes. Rejoicing meant standing tall in the face of discouragement, disappointment, and in my case, loneliness and boredom. But more than anything, rejoicing is biblical and a wild step of obedience in the face of hard-to-deal-with circumstances.

Disappointment—God's Reappointment

When things don't happen as we had planned, we face disappointment. This is normal. There is nothing wrong with being disappointed, but we must know what to do with that feeling or it will move into something more serious. In this world we will always have disappointment, but we can make the wild choice to believe and behave as if our disappointment is actually God's *reappointment*. It is God's recalculation and provision for us.

The apostle Paul had to learn how to live differently than he had been. To be a true follower of Christ, he had to confront the way he had lived before and everything he believed in. He spent the rest of his life and ministry teaching others how to live. I think one of the wildest things he has to say to us is this:

> But one thing I do [it is my one aspiration]: forgetting what lies behind and straining forward to what lies ahead, I press on toward the goal.
>
> Philippians 3:13–14 AMP

He showed us how to turn disappointment immediately into reappointment by pressing on to what lies ahead of us. When we let go, we get a new vision, plan, or idea; we get a fresh outlook, a new mind-set, and a change of focus.

Throughout the Bible, God instructs us to be filled with joy and to rejoice:

Rejoice in the Lord always [delight, gladden yourselves in Him]; again I say, Rejoice!

Philippians 4:4 AMP

Any time God tells us twice to do something—as he told the Christians in Philippi twice here—we'd better pay attention. The apostle Paul knew the power of rejoicing. He did it when he and Silas were in the Philippian jail:

About midnight, as Paul and Silas were praying and singing hymns of praise to God . . . suddenly there was a great earthquake, so that the very foundations of the prison were shaken; and at once all the doors were opened and everyone's shackles were unfastened.

Acts 16:25–26 AMP

Is that wild or what?

Rejoicing in the Lord is wild. It goes against the grain. Many times people see or hear the word *rejoice* and think it sounds nice, but they don't know how to do it. Rejoicing is an action that we do, and it can be as simple as singing, reading Scripture, laughing with friends, enjoying life, or looking for the good in all things. Rejoicing is a safeguard for us and an attitude adjuster. Rejoicing is also a choice.

The Treasure Hunt

Let's face it: sometimes we have to search for the sparkle. It's not always obvious. We have to look for good as if it were gold. We have to hunt for truth as if it were hidden treasure. Paul taught us that we are to look for the good and dwell there. I cannot tell you how many times I have had to ask myself, "What is good right now?" And sometimes I get too discouraged to even know or see.

I have made it a habit to surround myself with things that remind me of the "good" of God from my past experiences

171

with him. They help me to stay anchored in truth. Some of these things and what they remind me of are:

- a little jar of sand—his thoughts are more in number than the grains of sand
- a puzzle piece—all things, even every piece of my life, are working together for good
- a bowl of shells—God is the creator of all things, and his natural design is exquisite
- a bird's nest—he cares for the birds and tells me not to worry, because he cares for me
- sparkle frames—I should not "miss the sparkle"
- a framed picture of me with someone I admire—it is God who opens doors in our lives
- my old orthopedic boot with the sparkle pin—the journey of pain, rehabilitation, and gait training; God got my attention and should always get my praise
- a picture of me and my mother—reminding me to "live like it's real"

There are many more things, but these few give you an idea of what I am talking about. I want to celebrate the goodness of God, and I usually need reminding.

> Celebrate God all day, every day. I mean revel in him! . . . Summing it all up, friends, I'd say you'll do best by filling your minds and meditating on things true, noble, reputable, authentic, compelling, gracious—the best, not the worst; the beautiful, not the ugly; things to praise, not things to curse.
>
> Philippians 4:4, 8 Message

Release Your Joy

Sherrie made a choice to rejoice—and it changed her situation. It did not change the length of her days or the outcome of her illness, but it did change the quality of those days. She exhibited joy, and joy is a fruit of the Holy Spirit.

You might be thinking, *Well, that's nice for Sherrie. Good for her.*

But let me remind you that if joy is a fruit of the Spirit and the Spirit is in you, joy is in you. You're not trying to get joy or manufacture it; it is already there. We have joy. Joy is in our spirit; we need to learn how to release it, choose it, live in it.

The apostle Paul said:

> But none of these things move me; neither do I esteem my life dear to myself, if only I may finish my course with joy.
>
> Acts 20:24 AMP

According to Strong's concordance, the root of the Greek word, translated *joy* here, is cheerfulness and calm delight. The meanings of one Hebrew word for joy are "to rejoice, make glad, be joined." Another Hebrew word for joy can be translated "to spin around."

When we are joined with God, there is joy in our lives. Sometimes when things are discouraging, we need to rejoice whether we feel like it or not. I do this by telling myself the truth of God's promises out loud.

Many mornings I wake up and don't want to rejoice. My first thought is often *Ugh!* I quickly realize that and know that I have to turn it around. I make a choice then to begin thanking God for anything I can think of. I fight off discouragement at the onset through praise and thanks. I often sing.

Recently I have made a little "station" for myself in our office downstairs. I can close the doors, spend time in prayer, then put some music on and sing with it. This morning I was in a full-blown worship service led by Chris Tomlin, right there in my own home office with the doors shut. I raised my hands and smiled as I sang to God. And I kid you not, my entire attitude toward the day, my life, my pain, my deadlines, and my circumstances changed. Praising God is a miracle.

Praising God goes against the flesh. Looking to God is the pathway to dying to self, because we are admitting he is bigger than us and that we need him. We are also admitting that we can't make it on our own. We become dead to the self-life and alive to the Spirit's life within us.

Death to self is a wild idea. We are told to find ourselves, protect ourselves, and promote ourselves. But die to self? Wild.

Not only was Sherrie preparing for her eternal destination, she was also dying to her "Sherrie-self" and letting God be magnified in her. It was her earth's finale, and she lived it in spectacular fashion.

As we keep before us the clear and forceful vision of Jesus and his kingdom, we make daily progress. Our personality becomes increasingly reorganized around God. The substance of ourselves—formed in a world set against God—is always ready to act contrary to him in all of its dimensions. Our very habits of thinking, feeling, and willing are wrongly poised. But the one who is dead to self will not even notice some things that others would, such as social slights, verbal put-downs and innuendos, or physical discomforts. It's true, of course, that we will still notice—often quite clearly—many other rebuffs to "the dear self," but we will, as Saint Francis of Assisi said, "wear the world like a loose garment, which touches us in a few places there lightly."[2]

Born to Be Wild

I keep an undeveloped roll of 35 mm film on my desk.

Why? Because I am eccentric or a little kooky? Well, not really. I keep the film there to remind me of the potential that has been placed within me, for God's glory, since the time he formed me for his purposes. But like this roll of film, my life will not fulfill the plan that I was created for if it is left undeveloped. Development is the key—it is crucial, pivotal, and to be embraced.

Being in God's developing solution is a miracle too. He takes us, like a roll of film, and brings beauty to life—making the image of Christ within us come alive. He takes gray and makes color, takes black and white and makes sparkling hues. He takes what is blurry and brings it into focus. He crops the portrait to suit his plan. Oh, what a wonderful God we serve!

You and I were born to be wild. We were born for this hour of surrender, this day of being reconciled to the God who made us. Will you join me and say yes to the call to the wild side? You will never regret learning to trust God with the details of living. He and he alone can teach you how to live up rather than act out. Remember, anyone can act out. It takes a special someone to dig her heels into the truth and her heart into God—and learn to live up! It's all about a new groove—get your boogie on and take his hand to the dance floor! It's time to be wild for Jesus!

He is calling—I want to follow. How about you?

Wild Strategies for Capturing the Sparkle in Life

Look Up

- When hit with a real-life disappointment, trial, or hardship, stop and look up to acknowledge God.
- Search for anything to be thankful for, and thank him.
- Notice the good in everything and everyone.

Pray Up

- Take everything to the Lord in prayer.
- Refuse to be anxious.
- Pray and praise God instead.

Live Up

- If there is anything good, dwell on it!
- If there is anything good, speak it!
- If there is anything good, find it and be grateful!

Questions for Reflection on the Wild Life

1. Read Philippians 4:4–9. What does this say about finding the sparkle?
2. What good have you seen in your life lately?
3. How have you experienced the peace of God when dwelling on good things?
4. Would it be wild to be thankful even in the dark moments in life? How can you begin to do this?
5. Read Philippians 3:1 and 4:4. Why do you think Paul repeated the instruction to "rejoice" twice?

Parting Thoughts

*T*oday I am in Palm Springs, California. I am looking at a backdrop of majestically chiseled mountains and perfectly manicured palm trees set within a clear blue sky. It's a beautiful, humidity-free, eighty-degree day. The picture seems perfect.

As my husband and I took a walk around the resort grounds, a sign at the exit caught my eye. With big, bold graphic design, it says, "Buckle Up—Stay Fabulous!"

I laughed out loud; it just cracked me up. Who thought of that? I would expect such a sign to say "Buckle Up—Stay Safe," but the idea of choosing fabulous over safe got my attention. Quite frankly, it reminded me of what it is to live the wild life.

Life is not a picture-perfect day with no humidity and a beautiful backdrop. No, life is hard.

That is why we must remember to just "buckle up" and let our big, majestically mighty God sit in the driver's seat. And as for staying fabulous, remember, you are a new woman in Christ, and what makes you fabulous is Christ in you. Every day you are progressing from glory to glory as you are being changed into all that God has dreamed for you to be (see

2 Cor. 3:18). You are learning to live up instead of settling for acting out. Things are changing, baby step by baby step—and that is a beautiful pace. Take a breath, believe the truth, and embrace the process.

When you live buckled up with Jesus at the wheel, you stay fabulous, because you are walking and living in his Spirit instead of being in the driver's seat yourself. And as you relinquish the direction of your life, he then does his wild work in and through you. So I will close these pages with a charge to us all. *Wild women: buckle up and stay fabulous!*

And let's make a pact. Let's go through life saying the wild prayer:

> Less of me
>> Less of me
>>> Less of me
>>>> And much more of thee!

Study Guide

Chapter 1: Born to Be Wild

WILD is an acronym for Women in Lifelong Development. Throughout Scripture we are reminded that God is always working in us. He plans to develop us along the lines of his Son, Jesus. God is not as concerned with us being modern, educated, stylish, savvy women in the world we live in as he is committed to developing us into the godly, God-honoring, Spirit-led women he redeemed us to be.

1. Read Paul's words to the Colossians in Colossians 1:9–14.

What were Paul and Timothy asking God to do in the lives of the Colossians?

Fill them with the _____ of _____
through all _____ and
_____,
that they may live a life _____ of the Lord,
pleasing _____ in every way,
bearing fruit in every_____,
growing in _____,
being _____ with all _____
according to _____

to have _____ and patience
and give joyful thanks to the Father.

We often wonder how to pray for others, and often we are even lost when praying for ourselves. Far too often our prayers end up being lists of things we want God to do for us. But he is God, not an errand boy. And though he does want us to come to him with our requests, the most important thing he desires is to shape us, develop us, and form us into women who have these characteristics that Paul prayed for the Christians in Colosse.

Paul teaches us what is most important through how he prayed for them. Because we all have the same basic needs as we live this life, we should pray for others and pray for ourselves that we would:

- understand God's will
- grow spiritually
- honor and please God
- be filled with God's strength
- have endurance and patience through our daily struggles
- remain in the joy of Jesus Christ
- bear fruit that will last forever—eternal fruit

How does this prayer list differ from the one you usually recite?

Would it be wild to begin to get the focus off of externals and delve into a spiritual prayer pattern, such as Paul did here?

2. Read Colossians 1:13 again. What has God rescued you from?

The Colossians feared the forces of darkness and were superstitious about things unseen, but Paul says that true believers have been transferred from darkness to light, from slavery to freedom, from guilt to forgiveness, and from living under the power of Satan to living in the power of God. We have been rescued from a kingdom of rebel values. Our lives should begin to reflect this new allegiance—this is WILD living.

3. Write out Colossians 1:16–17.

How does this relate to your life? Who holds you together?

4. Read Colossians 1:19–23.

Verse 21 says you were once alienated from God. Alienated means estranged. How do you think growing up in this culture alienates us from God?

Think about what this passage is saying. You were once an enemy in your mind! Can you see the link here between what you think and what you do, between how you think and how you live? As we become more and more wild for Jesus, we will be conscious of the need to constantly have our minds renewed with truth. This mind renewal will in turn impact our behavior, which will affect the practical outcome of our lives.

5. Write out John 3:30.

Can you join with John the Baptist in praying this wild prayer? Why is this so wild? Because we are conditioned to make ourselves the leading ladies of our lives. To relinquish that willingly and actually ask to become less of "me" and more of "him" is countercultural and wild indeed.

6. Read James 2:14–26.

What does this say about being WILD?

Think of some times in your life when your faith was too tame or dead and without actions to back it up.

What can change that in the future?

Abraham believed God—he was wild—and it was counted to him as righteousness. He was even called God's friend. His faith made him wild enough to take his son to the altar.

Abraham's faith and actions worked together. God intervened and protected Isaac. What can we learn from this?

7. **You were born for a distinct purpose, and wrapped in that purpose is an underlying call to intimacy with God. Look up the word intimate in the dictionary and write its definition here.**

How can you take your relationship with God from a surface level relationship to an intimate encounter with the Creator of all things?

Chapter 2: Wild Women Live Beyond the Norm

Wild women think and live out of the box. What box? The box of perfection and performance. Rather than letting faith become something to check off a list, wild women are growing in an authentic walk with Christ. Like the saints of old, wild women are daring to be different, passionate, free, unconventional, and courageous.

1. **Look up the following words in a dictionary and a thesaurus:**

passionate:

free:

unconventional:

courageous:

Do these words describe your "norm" in your relationship with Jesus?

Summarize how the above words can describe a woman who is WILD for Jesus.

2. Read Romans chapter 12.

What stands out to you, at this time in your life, as the main theme of this chapter?

Paul moves the Romans from theological reasoning to the practical. In this chapter of Romans we see the guidelines Paul gives for living as people of wild faith in a fallen world.

3. Paul lays out some instructions:

Offer your body as _____.
This is your spiritual act of _____.
Do not conform _____ to the _____
   of the world.
Be _____ by the _____ of your
   mind.
This is God's good, _____, and _____
   will.

4. Look up conform and transformed in the dictionary. What do you think God is saying through these two powerful words?

5. Based on Romans 12:3–4, how are you to view yourself?

6. How have you experienced God's gifting in you? What is your responsibility with your God-given gifts?

7. Write out Romans 12:9–10 and commit them to memory—this is the essence of being WILD.
   a. Love sincerely
   b. Hate evil
   c. Be devoted to others
   d. Honor others above yourself

8. What does Romans 12:12 tell you to do?

Write out the wild prayer (John 3:30) and dare to say it aloud!

Chapter 3: Wild Women Live in Process, Not Perfection

We live in a world that is all about quick fixes, instant gratification, and perfect people. Trouble is, there is no such thing as a perfect person—and quick fixes don't last for long. As Christian women we need to embrace process over perfection. Process produces peace, because we acknowledge that we are not in a race to the finish but we are on a journey—only expected to live one day at a time. This journey was meant to be filled with joy as we trust our lives into the hands of God. When left to fend for ourselves and perfect ourselves, we are trapped in an endless cycle of self-focus, shame, or overachievement. Our lives become about self, not about Christ.

1. Write out Psalm 138:8.

2. Read Ephesians 2:1–10. What are the key points?

3. What does this passage say you and I used to follow?

We lived to _____ the cravings of our
_____.

We followed its _____ and _____.

Think about what this is saying. What do you know about your sinful nature?

Do you think it is natural to gravitate toward its desires still?

4. According to verses 4–5, what did God do for us?

5. According to verses 8–9, how are you saved? How do these verses describe salvation?

6. Write out Ephesians 2:10.

Who are you? _____

What were you created for? _____

Who has the blueprint, design, or plan? _____

Because of God's love and Christ's sacrifice, you live according to a new ABC structure:

A—Alive in Christ
B—Beautiful in him
C—Controlled by his Spirit

7. **Read Romans 8:28–29.**

What does verse 28 promise?

What does verse 29 say God is after?

How can you hold on to this for hope?

8. **Find something (an object, a Bible verse) to remind you of this chapter's lesson. What did God show you about the difference between process and perfection?**

Chapter 4: Wild Women Follow after God

From a young age we have learned how to follow after many things. Not many of us have learned how to follow hard after God. It is acceptable and expected that we, even as believers, will follow after our own dreams, desires, and plans in order to have our best life. It's time we make a wild shift in how we do things. Girls, we need to learn to follow after God.

1. **Look up follow in the dictionary. Does this describe the way you relate to and live toward Christ?**

2. **Read Matthew 4:18–19.**

Put this in your own words, making the verses your own call to follow. What would Jesus be calling you away from and calling you to?

3. Do you believe that Christ can make a difference in you? Explain.

Think about this: Jesus asked Peter and Andrew to leave their fishing business. He was calling them away from their productive trades to lead others to becoming productive spiritually. Isn't it interesting that they didn't debate or make excuses about why it was not a good time or a good idea but they simply followed him at once? What excuses do you usually make when Jesus asks you to follow him in another area of your life, another day in your play, another relationship that needs his touch?

4. Read Mark chapter 1.

Here we find the same story of the two fishermen. But as you read the entire chapter, what do you see characterized their experience of spiritual things once they left their nets and followed Christ?

We often assume that the disciples were great men of faith, always doing the "right" thing from the moment they heard the call to follow. We think they were unlike us—some kind of supernatural breed—but they weren't. They had to grow as all believers do. They too were in God's development plan.

5. Read Mark 14:43–50. What happened here?

Just hours earlier, these same disciples had vowed never to desert Jesus (see Mark 14:31). What does this say to you about the nature of humanity, which Christ chose to come dwell in and work through?

6. Read John 4:27–38.

What were the disciples surprised to find Jesus doing?

Are you ever surprised by how God chooses to work? Explain a time like that in your life.

7. Verse 32 speaks of food. What kind of food is this speaking of?

Spiritual nourishment is more than Bible study, prayer, and going to church. Spiritual nourishment comes from doing God's will and following after him. We are nourished by what we do as well as what we take in.

8. Write out John 17:4.

What did Jesus say brought God glory?

How can you accomplish his will for your individual life?

Following after Christ may be the hardest thing you ever set out to do. It's easy to attend church, but to follow after God is a death to our own way and a humbling of ourselves before a God we have faith in but cannot yet see. But following is necessary if we are ever going to experience something different.

Do you want a changed life? Then try something new.

Pray the wild prayer and ask God to give you the desire to follow only after him: "Less of me—more of thee!"

Chapter 5: Wild Women Choose to Love Others

Love is said to be the mark of those who follow Christ. Was this said by philosophers with dreamy thoughts of spirituality and religion? Or was it said by poets whose verses inspired their audiences? No, actually the idea that love is the mark of a believer came straight out of the Bible. Wild women are marked by love, infused with a love greater than their own. Wild women love more through every developing season of the journey.

1. Read 1 John 4:7–17.

Here are some key points:

- Love comes from God.
- Let us love one another.
- We do not know God if we do not love.
- Jesus came that we might live through him.
- We know and we rely on the love of God.
- God is love.
- Love is made complete in us, because in this world we are like him.

What do these key points mean to you as a wild woman?

2. Read 1 John 4:19–21.

Why do we love?

If we hate our brother, what does that make us?

What command have we been given?

3. Read Matthew 22:37–40.

What are the two most important commands, according to Jesus?

Why do you suppose he says to love others as we love ourselves?

4. Read 1 Corinthians 12:31–13:13.

What is the "most excellent way" that Paul is speaking of?

What are we compared to when we do not have love?

What does verse 11 say about growing up?

Do you think following the way of love is a step in growing up? Why? What does that look like in practical living?

5. Write out Romans 5:5.

God's love is a gift that we could never afford on our own. It is priceless, endless, unfailing, and empowering. Imagine that you are at your favorite department store and you see something you really want. The problem is, you don't have the money for it—the price is way too high. Then a caring friend buys the item, has it wrapped, and gives it to you. How would you respond? How would you feel? Thank God right now for giving you the gift you could never afford. Thank God that this gift of love is the very thing that wild women need to possess in order to follow the path that Jesus lays out for those who love him and choose to follow him. We follow—he makes the difference. It is love that enables us to say, "Less of me—more of thee!"

Chapter 6: Wild Women Forgive and Make Peace

Forgiveness is a gift we give ourselves. In many ways it is a self-ish choice because it frees us from self, increases the life-flow of God's Spirit in us, and sets us free to live in internal calm instead of chaos.

1. Read Matthew 18:21–35.

We are told to forgive our brother not _____ times but _____ times.

What does the rest of the story illustrate that you can apply to your own life?

How does it say the Lord God will treat those who refuse to forgive?

2. Read Colossians 3:12–14.

What are you called in verse 12?

What are you to clothe yourself in?

How are you to treat others?

How are you to treat those with whom you have a grievance?

What does love do, according to verse 14?

3. Write out John 10:27.

How have you been actively listening to God's voice in your relationships with others?

Are you following after God's way of forgiveness or giving way to anger and bitterness?

4. Read Proverbs 29:11.

How can you apply this wisdom to your life?

5. Read Proverbs 29:22.

What does an angry woman do?

What does a hot-tempered woman commit?

6. Read Hebrews 12:14–15.

What does this verse tell you to do? Explain it in your own words, and be specific.

God's way is not the world's way. It is a way that is often hard and requires us to do things we would rather not do (such as forgive, love, and turn the other cheek). But God's way is what we were created for. This new path is the wild journey of those who desire to sojourn with the Almighty.

Chapter 7: Wild Women Wear a Different Style

When was the last time you made a cutting remark to a friend about another woman? Maybe it was that she looked stuffed into her dress or tired out of her mind. Whatever it was, when you said it you tried on an ugly in-fit not fitting who you are as Christ's own. Over time, as the developing process continues, these uglies will get fewer and farther apart. We are called chosen women, and as such, we have a new wardrobe waiting for us—we just need to put on the truth, walk in the light, and live in God's love. This is wild!

1. Read Ephesians 4:22–25.

You were taught, in regard to your former ways, to:

Put _____ your old _____.
Be made _____ in the _____ of your mind.
Put on the _____ self, created to be like God in holiness.
Put off _____ and speak truth, for we belong to one another.

2. Ephesians 4:26 gives us some direct instruction. What is it?

3. According to Ephesians 4:29, what is not to come out of your mouth?

When was the last time something unedifying or unwholesome came out of you?

How can you change that "in-fit" so that your "in-fit" glorifies God and edifies others?

4. Write out Ephesians 4:32.

5. Read Ephesians 5:1–2.

What are we being told to do here?

What does this "in-fit" look like?

6. Read Galatians 5:16–23. These verses are key for learning what to take off and what to put on.

What are you to take off?

What are you to put on?

Wild women are called to sport the Jesus style. It is the fashion of a kind heart, the brilliance of a balanced mind, and the accessory of a life sprinkled with the touch and movement of God's Holy Spirit. But it doesn't happen by itself. We are told to put it on. We take off the old—and put on the new. This is the wild way to dress ourselves for life.

Chapter 8: Wild Women Worry Less and Trust More

This life gives us plenty to worry about. You don't have to go far to find something to cause anxiety or stress. But God in his love for us has called us to something really wild—and it's called trust. This kind of living can happen only when we begin to walk in faith, one step at a time. Often the steps are awkward, but if we keep stepping in the direction of truth, our lives begin to change and our footing begins to stabilize. The peace of God is more potent than any prescription medication, but we must learn to embrace it.

1. Read 1 Peter 5:6–10.

The first step in overcoming anxiety is to _____ourselves under God's _____.

The second step is to _____ our cares on _____.

What is the reason we can do this?

2. Scripture says we have an enemy (see 1 Pet. 5:8–9). What is he like?

How does the enemy try to devour you?

What are you to do when this happens?

Anxiety is often fear that has been exaggerated by the schemes of the enemy. He wants to convince you that God is not for you and that you are going under at any moment. You must stand firm, for God is a God of love, and he will always be faithful to you. It is quite wild to stand firm in the heat of things, but we can learn to be that wild!

3. Hebrews 11:1 defines faith. What is it?

4. Write out Hebrews 11:6.

Wild women believe two important things:

1. God exists.
2. He rewards those who seek him.

Have you sought him about whatever is making you anxious?

5. Read Hebrews 11:4–40.

What do these examples say to you about wild faith, trust, and surrender? Be specific.

6. Read James 1:5–7.

What does this tell you about faith in God in times of anxiety?

Chapter 9: Wild Women Stand Firm in Crisis

Every woman has crisis in her life. It might not be every day or every week, but there are seasons of change, crisis, disappointment, and other battles of living. Wild women look actively into God's Word to learn how to live in this real-life experience.

1. According to John 16:33, what does Jesus say is a sure bet in this life?

How are we to respond?

Why? What is Jesus's promise?

2. Read 2 Chronicles 20. This chapter is a road map for wild women in real-life battle.

How did King Jehoshaphat feel when he was told an army was coming up against him?

How do you generally feel when you receive bad news?

What did King Jehoshaphat do?

How is this different from what you usually do?

3. What instruction did the Lord give King Jehoshaphat in verse 15?

Do not _____ or _____.
For the _____ is not yours but
_____.

Think of a battle that you face. How could hearing this instruction from God help you?

Do you think there is power in having a different attitude—in choosing faith over fear?

4. **The people of Judah were told in verse 17 that they would not have to fight this battle but would have to:**

Take their _____, stand_____, and see the _____ of the Lord.

Look up these words in the dictionary and write their definitions below:

position:

firm:

deliverance:

5. **Praise was an important part of standing firm (see v. 21). What did the army sing as they headed out to battle?**

How would having this attitude and this "song" on your lips affect you today?

6. **What was the result of standing firm, singing praise, and trusting God (see v. 30)?**

7. **Read 2 Corinthians 4:8–9. Rewrite it in your own words.**

Chapter 10: Wild Women Confront Fear with Truth

Our minds often run away to places of negativity or fear. We are told throughout Scripture that we are to guard our minds and pay attention to what we are thinking. Rather than living randomly based on thinking randomly, wild women are learning to think purposefully, hopefully, and biblically. This is a challenge, but what is a wild life without a challenge, a dare, and a faith ride? Wild women fight fear with faith!

1. Read 2 Corinthians 10:1–7.

Paul is writing about our thought life. Let's break down what he is saying:

As Christ followers, we do not live by the _____ of the _____.

We do not wage _____ the way the _____ does.

We have different _____ that have divine _____.

We _____ arguments and every _____ that sets itself up against the knowledge of God.

We take _____ every _____ to make it obedient to Christ.

Take some time to think about what this is saying. Don't just skim or skip over this powerful instruction.

2. Look up the following words and write down their definitions:

standard:

weapons:

power:

pretension:

captive:

obedient:

As you read these definitions, what is God speaking to your heart about the passage in 2 Corinthians 10?

3. Look more closely at 2 Corinthians 10:7.

Can you see that there is a problem with only looking at the surface of things?

Does the surface of things sometimes bring your thoughts to places of fear and undermine the faith that you are trying to walk in?

What is the solution to this, according to this verse?

When was the last time that you considered or remembered that you belong to Christ?

Belonging to Christ is the most powerful truth for women who are committed to becoming WILD. Belonging is the foundation, the power, the promise, and the peace.

4. Read Proverbs 3:5–8.

This well-known passage should not be overlooked or minimized. It tells us a key to the wild life.

We are instructed to do a few things that are powerful:

_____ in the Lord with _____ your heart.

_____ not on your own _____.

In all your _____ acknowledge _____.

Do not be _____ in your own _____.

Fear the _____ and _____ evil.

These instructions are key to taking our thoughts captive!

5. What are we promised will result once we follow these directives (see v. 8)?

Think of a recent situation when you trusted your own thoughts and they led you down the wrong path in your thinking and actions. How could this have had a different outcome if you really lived like this passage says we should live?

6. Read Ephesians 6:10–15.

What is this saying to you about your thought life and the struggles you face as a woman today?

Remember this: our struggle, according to Scripture, is not against people! This is one belief that will cause you to live differently when faced with fear, problems, or what could ordinarily end up as girl drama. Wild women stand firm and put on the armor of God!

Chapter 11: Wild Women Have a New Groove

All of us have a familiar path, a reoccurring pattern, and a personal rhythm that we live in. If left unchallenged we would continue living in the pattern that comes naturally to our human flesh rather than challenging that groove and learning the new rhythm of the Spirit. One is death and the other is life. Wild women choose life!

1. Read 2 Peter 1:3–11. Some powerful stuff is packed in these verses.

What has given us everything we need for life?

How do we pave a new path toward godliness?

What have we been called to?

How do we escape living in our human nature?

2. Based on the above verses, what are our instructions for living?

Make every _____ to add to your _____
goodness;

add to goodness, _____;

and to knowledge, _____;

and to self-control, _____;

and to perseverance, _____;

and to godliness, _____;

and to kindness, _____.

What will these qualities produce in you and protect you from?

3. What happens to the woman who does not possess these (see v. 9)?

Do you ever forget you were cleansed from past sins?

What will keep you from falling?

4. Write out Psalm 138:8.

5. Now write out Psalm 138:8 in your own words, as a prayer of thanksgiving.

6. Read Galatians 5:1 and 5:16.

What message are you getting about living in a new wild groove?

Chapter 12: Wild Women Capture the Sparkle in Life

All of us can see life as a half-empty glass. It takes some discipline to turn our vision around so we become women who see the glass as half full rather than half empty. It's the same glass, isn't it? But there are two ways to view it. Wild women learn to see the sparkle, the beauty, the good in their lives, in others, and in their situations. There are many things we cannot change, and there is much we have no control over, but we do get to choose the attitude we carry with us each day.

1. Read Acts 16:16–34.

What are the key points to this story of Paul and Silas?

2. According to this passage, what were Paul and Silas doing at midnight?

Why were they doing what they were doing?

What was the result of their praise?

We all have times when we feel we are locked up or imprisoned in our trials or circumstances. Think of a "prison cell" time in your own life. Did you even think of praising God? What might have been different if you had?

3. Read 1 Thessalonians 5:16–22.

Here are the key ingredients to capturing the sparkle in life:

Be _____ always;

_____ continually;

give _____ in _____ circumstances.

What are those three things said to be (v. 18)?

When in doubt of God's will, recapture the sparkle and the excitement of living as one belonging to Christ by practicing the above model.

4. Read Philippians 4:4–8.

What is the next ingredient in capturing the sparkle?

Write out Philippians 4:6 and commit it to memory.

5. Concentrate now on Philippians 4:8.

What is this verse telling you to do?

Imagine a treasure hunt. How can you look for the good?

6. Now look at Philippians 4:11. What did Paul learn?

Do you think capturing the good or the sparkle was part of that?

Do you think praising instead of complaining aided that attitude of contentment?

7. Finally, write out Philippians 4:13.

This verse, often memorized by young and old alike, can be life changing if remembered in the context of all that came before it in Philippians chapter 4. Paul learned how to live in every and any situation: he learned to be content and believed he could do all things presented to him—in Christ's strength. This is a wild way to look at life, to live life, and to glorify God in this life. It is also a wild way to shine as stars in his universe, holding out the word of truth to all those who don't know him (see Phil. 2:14–16).

8. **Philippians 4:19 is a promise for the wild woman. What does it promise?**

When we believe that God is our total provision in this life, we change. I will be the first to admit that believing this truth in hard times is difficult. But, that is what is wild about believing truth. To believe truth doesn't mean we have to totally understand it—we learn to accept it and embrace it.

Notes

Part 1: Developing

1. Chris Tomlin, foreword to *Crazy Love* by Frances Chan (Colorado Springs: David C. Cook, 2008), 4.

Chapter 1: Born to Be Wild

1. Rick Warren, Purpose Driven Life Daily Devotional, July 25, 2008, purpose drivenlife.com.
2. Rick Warren, "Becoming Like Jesus Is a Slow Process," Purpose Driven Life Daily Devotional, purposedrivenlife.com.
3. Francis Chan, *Crazy Love* (Colorado Springs: David C. Cook, 2008), 44.

Chapter 2: Wild Women Live Beyond the Norm

1. Michelle Borquez, *God Crazy* (Eugene, OR: Harvest House, 2007), 13.
2. Matthew Henry Commentary (Grand Rapids: Zondervan, 1960), 1950.
3. Ken Gire, *The Divine Embrace* (Wheaton: Tyndale, 2003), 31.

Chapter 3: Wild Women Live in Process, Not Perfection

1. Oswald Chambers, *My Utmost for His Highest* (Grand Rapids: Discovery House, 1992), May 8.
2. Ibid., June 15.

Chapter 4: Wild Women Follow after God

1. Eugene Peterson, *A Long Obedience in the Same Direction* (Downers Grove, IL: InterVarsity, 2000), 65.

2. Kitty Crenshaw and Catherine Snapp, *The Hidden Life* (Colorado Springs: NavPress, 2006), 123.

3. Ken Gire, *The Divine Embrace* (Wheaton: Tyndale, 2003), 27.

4. Oswald Chambers, *My Utmost for His Highest* (Grand Rapids: Discovery House, 1992), June 16.

5. Chris Tomlin, foreword to *Crazy Love* by Frances Chan (Colorado Springs: David C. Cook, 2008), 4.

Part 2: Daring

1. Dallas Willard, *Revolution of Character* (Colorado Springs: NavPress, 2005), 42.

Chapter 5: Wild Women Choose to Love Others

1. Max Lucado, *Just Like Jesus* (Nashville: Word, 1998), 46.

2. Chan, *Crazy Love*, 103.

3. Nancy Missler, *The Key* (Corte Alene, ID: Kings Highway Ministries, 2000), 20.

4. C. S. Lewis, *The Four Loves* (New York: Harcourt Brace Jovanovich, 1960).

5. Missler, *The Key*, 20.

6. Eugenia Price, quoted in Words to Warm the Heart Calendar (Siloam Springs, AR: Blessings Unlimited, 2001).

7. Oswald Chambers, July 28.

Chapter 6: Wild Women Forgive and Make Peace

1. Mother Teresa, www.writespirit.net/authors/motherteresaquotes.

2. C. S. Lewis, *Mere Christianity* (New York: Harper, 1952).

3. Nancy McGuirk, *Rest Assured* (Nashville: Broadman and Holman, 2008), 110.

4. Henry Cloud and John Townsend, *12 Christian Beliefs That Can Drive You Crazy* (Grand Rapids: Zondervan, 1995), 75.

5. Beth Moore, *Praying God's Word Devotional* (Nashville: Broadman and Holman, 2006), July 28.

Chapter 7: Wild Women Wear a Different Style

1. Chan, *Crazy Love*, 113.

2. Oswald Chambers, *My Utmost for His Highest*, June 17.

3. Ibid.

Chapter 8: Wild Women Worry Less and Trust More

1. Hannah Whitall Smith, *The Christian's Secret of a Happy Life* (Grand Rapids: Revell, 1985), 150.

Chapter 9: Wild Women Stand Firm in Crisis

1. McGuirk, *Rest Assured*, 62.
2. Ibid., 128.
3. Lorri Steer, "Wise Living for Today," www.lorriscancerupdate.blogspot
.com, July 30, 2008.
4. Life Application Study Bible sidebar.
5. Oswald Chambers, *My Utmost for His Highest*, November 24.

Chapter 10: Wild Women Confront Fear with Truth

1. Willard, *Revolution of Character*, 89.
2. Ibid., 88.
3. Ibid., 43.

Chapter 11: Wild Women Have a New Groove

1. Moore, *Praying God's Word*, 22.
2. Eugene Peterson, *A Long Obedience*, 120.
3. Gire, *The Divine Embrace*, 7.
4. Robert Boyd Munger, *My Heart—Christ's Home* (Downers Grove, IL: InterVarsity, 1992).
5. Crenshaw and Snapp, *The Hidden Life*, 123.

Chapter 12: Wild Women Capture the Sparkle in Life

1. Moore, *Praying God's Word*, 152.
2. Saint Francis of Assisi, quoted in Willard, *Revolution of Character*,
64–65.